i

HUMAN RESOURCES MANAGEMENT

HUMAN RESOURCES MANAGEMENT

Gabriel C. Ortigoza

To Gamiel, and Gamaliel...

Dream big and soar high but keep your feet on the ground

Table of Contents

PREFACE

One of the major courses offered to the school of management in Human Resources Management. HRM is a dynamic field in management that HR personnel needs a regular update to be in the loop.

This book came into being as my contribution to society based on research and experience as a Human Resources Management instructor to the graduating cadets at the Philippine Military Academy and my involvement in the procurement of PMA cadets and as proctor of PMA Entrance Examination in the academy's annual national procurement of cadets.

This book aims to explain the basic concepts, theories, functions, and principles unique to human resources management and to understand the issues, problems, and realities of managing human resources in government organizations to include civilian and military institutions and to non-government organizations.

Human Resources Management is valuable to anyone dealing with people or aspiring to have a professional career in personnel management.

ACKNOWLEDGEMENTS

The author would like to recognize the following persons for inspiration in writing this book:

Brigadier General Mario G. Lacurom (PMA '85) of the Philippine Army for inviting the author to join the teaching pool as a guest instructor of the Department of Management at PMA. Brig. Gen. Lacurom was then a major in 1997 when he recruited the author, who was then a young first lieutenant, to teach management courses to PMA cadets and for sharing materials pertinent to Human Resources Management.

Secretary Delfin N. Lorenzana (PMA '73) of the Department of National Defense for the immediate action and approval of the author's letter request in 2016 to include the Province of Cotabato (author's province) as one of the testing sites for PMA Entrance Examination in the annual nationwide procurement of cadets.

To the author's family: Gemma, Gamiel, and Gamaliel for the love and support.

And above all, to God Almighty for the knowledge and wisdom bestowed upon the author in writing this book.

INTRODUCTION

People constitute an organization's most important and vital factor in its success or failure. Human Resources Management (HRM) consists of researches involved in the science and art of managing the most important resources of an organization – the people.

This book comprises of managerial and personnel operative functions vital to accomplish organizational goals and objectives. HRM gives special attention to how human resource management practices can influence productivity and quality of work life. By analyzing personnel management practices in terms of these two critical organizational outcomes, managers are empowered to apply human resources management concepts in a way that delivers positive strategic influence on the success of the organization.

Human resource is pervasive in all types of organization whether public or private, regardless of size, function, or type of activity. Because human resources are a major asset of an organization, taking in people requires a careful study of the present as well as the future demands of public administration including the personnel needed to carry out responsibilities and perform required services.

There are other organizational needs like the physical plant, equipment, and money but the human resource is the most crucial determinant of the success or failure of an enterprise. The organization may have good plans, orderly sequenced workflow, symmetrically pattern of organization, efficient fiscal control system but may yet be a failure by employing the wrong people and not motivating them.

The challenge of management is not so much in its money, machines, methods, and markets but its people. The quality of the utilization of the latter is almost always affected by a decision about human resources. If the bottom line of the organization is to get results, it must hire the right people.

Chapter I

HUMAN RESOURCE MANAGEMENT

Human Resources Management is defined as a formal system designed to managed people in an organization. Managing people ultimately has to do with the decisions these leaders made from among the wide range of possible choices on the formal policies, practices, and methods used (Cursa). It consists of personnel operative functions of procurement, development, compensation, integration, maintenance, and records.

Human Resource Objectives

1. Provide stable employment, equitable compensation, desirable working conditions, and opportunities for advancement for employees in return for their skill, care effort, dependability, and teamwork.
2. Create a climate conducive to the development of each employee by his needs, interest, desires, abilities, and willingness to take additional responsibility.
3. Manage human resources to ensure continuing vitality and growth to the company while realizing a profit and providing opportunities for public services.
4. Deliver enlightened leadership to ensure maximum work satisfaction for each employee in a centralized or decentralized environment.
5. Define clearly for each individual the responsibilities of his position to enable him to make his best contribution to overall organizational goals.

Human Resource Planning

An organization must devise effective procedures to ensure that its staffing needs are being met. Human resource planning is important for helping both organizations and employees to prepare for the future. But you might be asking, "Aren't things always changing?" So, what is the value of planning? The answer is that even an imperfect forecast of the future can be quite helpful. Even if such forecast or prediction can sometimes be wrong, it is better than no forecast or prediction at all. The key is whether one's predictive tool improves the chances of making the right decisions. Even though the predictive tool may not be accurate, as long as it is more accurate than random guessing, it will result in a better decision.

The same point applies to human resource planning. Even though neither organizations nor employees can see into the future, making predictions can be quite helpful, even if they are not always accurate. The basic goal then of human resource planning is to predict the future and based on these predictions, implement programs to avoid anticipated problems.

Human resource planning as defined by different personnel management authors:

Human resource planning is a process by which management ensures that it has the right number and kinds of people at the right places, and at the right times, who are capable of effectively and efficiently completing those tasks that will help the organization achieve its overall objectives. Human resource planning, then, translates the organization's objectives into terms of the workers needed to meet those objectives (Robbins, 1988).

Human resource planning, also known as manpower planning, is a process of analyzing an organization's human resource needs under changing conditions and developing the activities necessary to satisfy these needs. It is a dynamic management process of ensuring that at all times, a company or its unit has in it employ the right number of people, with the right skills and assigned to the right jobs where they can contribute most effectively to the productivity and profitability of the company. Human resource planning is concerned with the efficient acquisition and maximum utilization of the company's human resources to enable the company to attain its goals and objectives (Sison, 1991).

Human Resource Planning is further defined as the process of systematically reviewing the human resource requirements to ensure that the required number of employees with the required skills are available when they are needed (Mondy, et. at., 1993).

Human Resource Planning describes the intended actions of the organizations to ensure that that the organization has the right number and the right mix of people at the right time and place to achieve efficiently present and future organizational goals (Lawrence, et. al., 1985).

Human resource planning is the process of examining an organization's or individual's future human resource needs (for instance, what types of skill will be needed for the jobs of the future) compared to future human resource capabilities (such as the types of skills employees you already have) and developing human resource policies and practices to address potential problems (for example, implementing training programs to avoid skill deficiencies) (Harris, 1997).

Importance of Human Resource Planning

Although human resource planning has a large impact on organizational effectiveness, its importance is often overlooked. Human resource planning accompanies and supports the strategic business plans; to reach its long-term goals, an organization must have the proper mix of employees with the necessary knowledge, skills, and abilities. The human resource planning process precedes recruitment and selection activities and provides the foundation for personnel staffing. Before new employees are recruited, someone needs to decide what kinds of employees are need and how many, and these decisions need to be aligned with the organization's strategic business plans. Hiring new employees should be based on the projected staffing requirements if the projection indicates a demand for new employees, recruiting activities should be initiated if it indicates a surplus of personnel, early retirements, layoffs, or other actions may be necessary.

Basic Approach to Human Resource Planning

Human Resource Planning at the company level is concerned with the following: the people needed to assist the company /firm/organization and each operating unit in meeting its goals and objectives thru planning for the effective, economical use of human resources, the inventory of available human resource supply within and outside the organization to identify human resource needs for the total organization and initiate plans to meet them, the identification of gaps in matching human resource with the demand of jobs and design programs to bridge the gaps, the preparation of programs for productivity, growth, and development of people, the provision of systems and procedures that will maximize the utilization of human time and potential, and the furnishing of the environment what is necessary to attract and retain productive people.

Stephen Robbins explains job analysis, job description, and job satisfaction:

Job Analysis

While the human resource inventory is concerned with telling management what individual employees can do, job analysis is more fundamental. It defines the jobs within the organization and the behaviors necessary to perform these jobs.

Job Description and Job Specification

The job description is a written statement of what a jobholder does, how it is done, and why it is done. It should accurately portray job content, environment, and conditions of employment. The job specification states the minimum acceptable qualifications that an incumbent must possess to perform a given job successfully. It identifies the knowledge, skills, and abilities needed to do the job effectively.

Job description and job specification are important documents when managers begin recruiting and selecting. The job description can be used to describe the job to potential candidates. The job specification keeps the manager's attention on the list of qualifications necessary for an incumbent to perform a job and assists in determining whether candidates are qualified.

Implementing new human resource programs often sounds much easier than it is because employees tend to resist change. Choosing and implementing programs is a critical component in the human resource planning process. Because organizational resistance can defeat even the most effective programs, special attention must be paid to ensure that the program is accepted by all affected parties.

Human Resource Planning Process

As has been defined earlier, Human Resource Planning is the process of systematically reviewing human resource requirements to ensure that the required number of employees with the required skills are available when they are needed. Furthermore, it is the process of matching the internal and external supply of people with job openings anticipated in the organization over a specified period.

Strategic Planning - Corporate Level Planning

The first step in the planning process is the determination of overall organizational purposes and objectives and how they are achieved. Essentially, human resource planning should be linked to organizational strategy.
Top management sets the tone for the development of strategy formulation and the Human Resource Planning department's role, in turn, will be to raise issues relative to the treatment of employees.

According to some surveys of top-level executives, the best methods of improving quality and overall productivity are directly related to human resource issues. Motivation, culture, and education were related to the best methods for increasing productivity.

Employees must be adequately motivated, prepared to deal with the existing corporate culture, and appropriately educated to cope with the challenges of their jobs.

After organizational goals and strategic plans have been formulated, Human Resource Planning may be undertaken. Strategic plans are reduced to specific quantitative and qualitative human resource plans.

Forecasting Human Resource Requirements - involves determining the number and type of employees needed, by skill level and location. These projections will reflect various factors such as production plans and changes in productivity.

Forecasting Human Resource Availability - Human Resource managers should look at both external and internal sources (labor market and presently employed workers).

When Human Resource Requirements and Availability has been analyzed, the company can determine whether it will have a surplus or shortage of workers. Ways and means must be found to reduce the number of employees if the SURPLUS is projected. Some of the methods are restricted hiring, reduce Hours (working hours), early retirement, and layoffs.

If a shortage is forecasted, the firm or company must obtain the proper quantity and quality of workers from outside the organization (labor market). External recruitment and selection are required.

Intermediate Planning Level

Modem corporations especially multinational corporations have grown so large that they must group subsidiaries into divisions or sectors or departments. For strategic purposes, special groupings of operations into a single product market group called Strategic Business Unit (SBU) is used. (Lawrence, et. al., 1985)

The intermediate level of planning within the company deals with entrepreneurial growth and change in the firm in terms of product and markets.

The HR department must prepare fairly specific three-year plans for all its activities to support the major changes in the firm's development. It must also prepare the most specific plans for acquiring future managers, key personnel, and the total number of employees in support of the company requirements over the next three years.

If a new company is to be acquired (expansion), plans for inter-granting the "culture" of the new company, the policies, labor contracts, training, compensation, benefits, etc. must be prepared.

On the other hand, if a company is to be divested or sold by the firm, the Human Resource Department must have plans for separation, transfer, or restoration of key people.

Operations Planning

At the lowest business center levels, the one-year operating plans are the blueprints for the year ahead. Detailed monthly forecasts of sales, revenues, expenses, as well as planned accomplishments and utilization of human and material resources, are documented.

Human Resource Planning at this level includes detailed plans for all Human Resource activities. These plans are designed to support the manpower requirements of other managers throughout the company.

Short-term Activities Planning

This refers to varied short terms planning from one (1) day to ten (10) months problems. Example: Replacement of unskilled workers who leave the company; the handling of employee benefits, the review of accident reports; and the processing of union grievances are required to support short-term company activities.

Human Resource Management Operative Functions

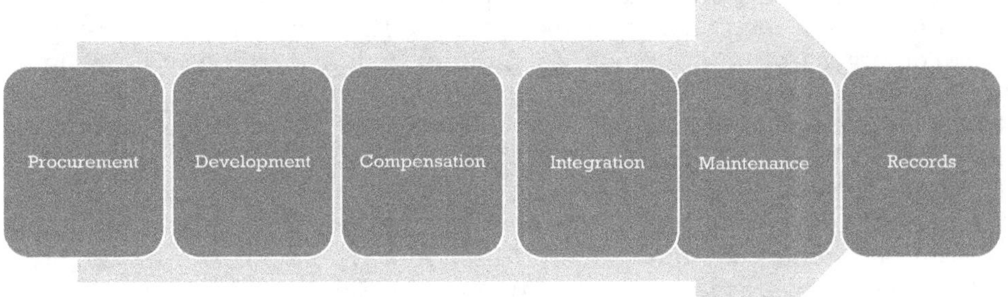

Chapter II

PROCUREMENT

When I was in the Corps of Professors at the Philippine Military Academy, I was involved in the annual national procurement of PMA cadets. I served several times as proctor of PMA Entrance Examination; and in 2001, I was appointed as Officer-In-Charge of special PMAEE given to the cities of Davao, General Santos, Koronadal, and Cotabato. I also brought PMAEE to my hometown in Mlang in Cotabato Province (formerly North Cotabato) for the first time. In 2016, I wrote a letter to Defense Secretary Delfin Lorenzana asking the good secretary to include my province as a testing site in the annual PMAEE. Secretary Lorenzana immediately approved my request and directed PMA Superintendent to include Cotabato Province as one of the official sites nationwide of PMAEE. Since then, qualified youths from my province has been included in the annual procurement of PMA cadets. I am proud to tell you that some of the qualified youths from my province were successful in their quests to become cadets and now officers of the armed forces of the Philippines.

What is procurement? Procurement is the determination of manpower needs to analyze each job to determine the nature of the work, the qualifications necessary, the nature and amount of training required, the amount of supervision necessary; to derive from the job analysis and job specifications containing in condensed form the most pertinent points relating to the position and the worker, to be used by employment interviews to facilitate the work of selection and placement; and to determine the manpower needs of the organization (yourarticlelibrary.com).

Human resource is pervasive in all types of organization, whether public or private, regardless of size, function, or type of activity. Because human resources are a major asset of an organization, taking in people requires a careful study of the present as well as the future demands of the public administration environment including the personnel needed to enable it to carry out responsibilities and perform required services. There are other organizational needs like a physical plant, equipment, and money but the human resource is the most crucial determinant of the success of failure of an enterprise. The organization may have good plans, orderly sequenced workflow, symmetrically drafted pattern of organization, efficient fiscal control system but may yet be a failure by employing the wrong people and not motivating them. If the bottom line of the organization is to get results, it must hire the right people (Tendero, 1995).

Staffing positions in organizations may well represent one of the most important human resources management functions. Who is hired into the job ideally reflects job-relevant decisions and the maximizing of critical knowledge, skills, and abilities which contribute to an organization's overall effectiveness and its competitive advantage? (Ferris, 1996).

After the need for personnel has been determined, several candidates may have to be recruited. This involves attracting qualified candidates to fill organizational roles. From this, potential personnel are selected: this is the process of choosing from among the candidates the most qualified one. The aim is to place people in positions where they can utilize their strengths, and perhaps overcome their weaknesses by getting experience or training in those skills in which they need improvement. Finally, placing personnel into a new position within the organization often results in a promotion; which normally involves more responsibility (Koonts, 1980).

Procurement is composed of three important processes of Human Resources Management: recruitment, selection, and placement.

Recruitment

Recruitment is the search for employees both inside or outside the organization to fill vacant positions. When there are not enough internal candidates so that the organization must look outside. An important objective is to obtain highly qualified employees at the lowest effective cost.

The term recruitment refers to the practices of an organization to persuade people to apply for employment in the company while the selection is the process of determining who from among the job applicants should get the job. Placement is the function of making a new employee familiar with his new job and work environment (Abasolo, 1991).

Purpose of Recruitment

The purpose of recruitment is to provide enough group of candidates so that the organization will be able to select the qualified employees that it needs. General recruiting takes place when the organization needs a group of workers of a certain kind, this is most appropriate for operative employees e.g. typists or salespeople. Specialized recruiting is used mainly for higher-level executives or specialists, which occurs when the organization desires a particular type of individual. In specialized recruiting, candidates receive personalized attention over an extended period, e.g. recruiting professionals.

Source for Recruitment

Recruitment takes place within the labor market — that is people available with the skills needed to fill the positions open in the organization. The labor market changes over time in response to environmental factors.

The sources to which the human resources department turns to meet their recruitment needs depends upon the availability of the right people in the local labor pool, as well as on the nature of the positions to be filled. An organization's ability to recruit employees often depends as much on the organization's reputation and the attractiveness of its location as on the attractiveness of the specific job offer. If the people with the appropriate skills are not available in the organization itself or the local labor pool, they may have to be recruited from competing organizations and/or from some distance away.

For many types of jobs at every level, private employment agencies and newspaper "Help Wanted" advertisements are important sources for letting the local job market know an opening exists. "Employment Opportunities" advertisements in trade and professional journals, as well as communication directly with social and professional organizations, are important sources of recruitment of middle and upper-level people.

Of all methods of locating potential employees, the most often used and the most successful is word of mouth. In most organizations, more workers at every level are introduced to the firm through personal contact. In any individual career, more employment opportunities are likely to have been found through personal recommendation and referral. For the individual, developing a wide range of personal contacts and "networking" may be the most useful career planning activities.

Sources of Applicants

Internal Source of recruitment from within the organization itself is the first and easiest source because of its firsthand knowledge of its workers who have been tried and tested. Using this source saves recruitment, screening, and selection expense on the part of the organization. Furthermore, recruitment for within increases the general level of morale of employees.

Method Used in Recruitment

Job Posting - wherein every time a position becomes available it is offered to present employees before recruiting via outside sources. The job description is posted in one or more centrally located places. Include also the closing date by which time all applicants must be submitted.

External Source - This source is mainly tapped when the positions whose job specifications cannot be met by existing personnel. When the organization plans to expand and present personnel cannot be given overload without sacrificing the quality of their work new hires are needed.

Types of External Sources

Educational Institutions — Colleges and universities give free placement services to their graduates and prospective employers. Job announcements are posted on their bulletin boards and a list of graduating students are sent of sold out to organizations. Representatives of the organizations come to the school campus to interview and/or give tests to applicants. It is cheaper to let the recruiter visit the campus applicants than going to the organization.

Recommendations of Present Staff - By word of mouth to their relatives and friends, existing personnel announce job openings and recommend to management those whom they consider would qualify.

Walk-in Applicants - Applications come unsolicited and are given personally or are sent by mail by casual applicants.

Leasing - To avoid financial obligations like pensions, insurance, and other fringe benefits, some organizations hire people contractual jobs and get well-trained personnel. In the Philippines, security guards, maintenance personnel, and secretarial staff are hired by many organizations through this leasing source.

Employer's Families - Hiring family members or relatives is commonly done by family-owned firms and maybe hiring employees who do not merit the positions. The Civil Service Law of the Philippines prohibits employment of relatives within the third degree.

Office Files of Past Applicants - Application forms of those not hired at once place in the files for easy reference.

Most Common Method Used

Advertising. This is the display of vacant positions in advertisements. This is very popular for very practical reasons. It is relatively inexpensive and effective over some time. Another reason is that people seem natural to turn recruitment ads when looking for a job.

Factors Affecting Recruitment

Size of the Organization - the bigger the organization, the more positions are needed and so the Human Resources Department has to recruit applicants not only for existing vacancies and also for future exigencies as well.

Availability of Funds - recruitment needs a lot of funding if the organization wants to reach out to too many groups in and out of the country. These include the cost of hiring employment agencies as well as its advertisements and other sources of recruitment.

Image of the Organization - it speaks for itself, an organization with a very good image in most aspects (compensation program, labor-management relation, facilities) attracts more recruits.

Advantages and Disadvantages of the Various Recruitment Sources

Recruitment Source	Advantages	Disadvantages	Level of Position
Job Posting	Creates openings as lower, easier-to all levels Serves time and money	Managers feel they can no longer find persons of their choice	Nonexempt and exempt
Word of Mouth	Inexpensive Expeditious Related bonus boosts employee morale	May promote changes of systematic discrimination if not used in conjunction with other recruitment sources	Nonexempt and exempt
Advertising	Reaches a wide audience Can solicit responses via blind	Can be very costly Can delay the filling of positions	Employment agencies nonexempt search firm

	ads		exempt
Employment agencies and search firms	Access to large pools Can help fill a position quickly	Can refer unqualified applicants	Walk-ins, call-ins, and write-ins
Campus recruiting	No cost Good public relations	If on a manual system, can be time-consuming Poor notes taken by the previous interviewer may cloud applicant desirability	Nonexempt and exempt
Job fairs	No cost Good public relations	A poorly monitored system can result in lost applicants Interviewing walk-ins and talking with call-ins can disrupt interviewers work schedule	Walk-ins and call-ins nonexempt and exempt
	Opportunity to groom and develop future management of a company Opportunity to select top graduates	Costly Fatigue Must evaluate potential, as opposed to concrete work experience	Exempt
	May fill many openings in a short period	Costly Usually means working on a weekend	Exempt

Recruitment and Decruitment

Once managers know their current personnel status (whether they are understocked or overstocked), they can begin to do something about it. If one or more vacancies exist, they can use the information gathered through job analysis to guide them in recruitment – that is, the process of locating, identifying, and attracting capable applicants. On the other hand, if human resources planning indicates a surplus, management will want to reduce the labor supply within the organization. This activity, according to Robbins, is called decruitment.

Decruitment Options

Option	Description
Firing	Permanent involuntary termination.
Layoffs	Temporary involuntary termination; may last only a few days or extend to years.
Attrition	Not filling openings created by voluntary resignation or normal retirements.
Transfers	Move employees either laterally or downward; usually does not reduce costs but can reduce Intra organizational supply-demand imbalances.
Reduced Workweeks	Employees work fewer hours per week, share jobs, or perform their jobs on a part-time basis.
Early Retirements	Incentives are provided to older and more senior employees for retiring before their normal retirement date.

Selection

Selection is that activity in which the organization uses one or more methods to assess individuals to decide their suitability to join that organization (Bolton, 1997). It is the process of determining which job candidates' best suit organizational needs. During the process of selection, managers must determine the extent to which job candidates have the skills, abilities, and knowledge required to perform effectively in the position for which they are being considered (Bartol, 1991). The selection process involves mutual decision making. The organization decides whether or not to make the job offer and how attractive the offer would be. The job candidate decides whether the organization and the job offer will fit his needs and goals (Stoner, 1989).

There are cases though when the selection process becomes one-sided. First, when the job market is extremely tight wherein several candidates will be applying for each position, and the organization will be based on a series of screening devices, hire the candidate that it feels more suitable. The process is also one-sided when the candidate is a highly qualified executive or professional who is being courted by several organizations.

Basis for Selection

The basis for selection should be the job description and job specification. If constant reference is not made to these documents throughout the selection process, it is easy to forget that what is required is not to select the "best" person but the "best person for the job", in other words, the one who most exactly fits the characteristics outlined in the job description and the person specification.

Reception of Applicant

Not all applicants are allowed to go through the entire process of selection. Some of them are eliminated through the "preliminary screening" or "sight screening" whereby the undesirable applicants are quickly eliminated based on a rapid appraisal of their apparent characteristics such as age, height, years of experience, physical condition, educational attainment, etc.

Screening is the process by which the applicants are interviewed and classified under two categories: those to be given examinations and further interviews and those who should not be considered at all.

Categories of Employees

Regular or permanent employee - is a person who has passed through a probationary period of employment. In short, he is employed with the company without a definite period and cannot be terminated except for a just cause.

Employment without a definite period - an employee has been hired without any specific date of termination or period of employment.

Probationary employee - is a person hired to occupy a permanent or regular position in the company for a specified trial period to prove if he is acceptable for the job.

Temporary employee - is a person hired to perform work in a specific project, job, or period, upon completion of which the worker's employment is terminated.

Contractual employee - is one hired on an individual employment contract basis to perform work on a specific project.

Casual employee - is one who is hired for only a few days or a few months at a time to perform a unit of work or to fill a gap in the absence of another employee, or the one who is hired occasionally and intermittently especially during peak production periods.

Objectives of Recruitment and Selection

To develop different sources of supply of applicants for different jobs, to design a standard requisition blank for use by operating department in requesting personnel, to design an application blank for each category of employees, to interview applicants by a trained interviewer, to introduce a testing program to supplement the interview, and to thoroughly investigate and medically examine successful applicants before employment (Chand, 2020)

Human Resource Recruitment and Selection Procedure

Organizational practice differs as to the recruitment and selection procedure for personnel used. In some small organizations, this may simply mean a face-to-face meeting between the owner and the job applicant. The owner may ask for some information and documents such as police clearance, biographical data, transcript of school records. Some questions may also be asked. The owner makes the decision either to employ or not. When the owner decides to hire the job applicant and the later starts working in the company, the recruitment and selection process is over.

Placement
The objectives of placement are to introduce a uniform procedure for introducing new employees to the company and the respective departments, provide employees copy of rules and regulations, and the department head or the supervisor to designate a fellow employee to escort newcomer during the first several days and to act as his "sponsor" (Chand, 2020).

Placement is the assignment of individuals to jobs. Furthermore, it is the optimal matching of employee talents with organizational needs. In large firms, for example, individuals may be selected initially based on their potential to succeed in general management.

In some organizations though, employees are selected specifically to fill certain positions. These are the so-called one-shot-selection-placement programs. In this case, placement becomes incorporated in the selection process.

Like the selection, placement also is a two-way process. A firm would want to make the most of the employee's talents, skills, and capabilities and thus would "place" him or her in a job where he could be most productive and efficient. On the other hand, an employee would tend to be more productive under working conditions favorable to him. Thus, placement is important in that it could spell the difference between success and failure of the organization in terms of efficiency and productivity.

Two Way Process

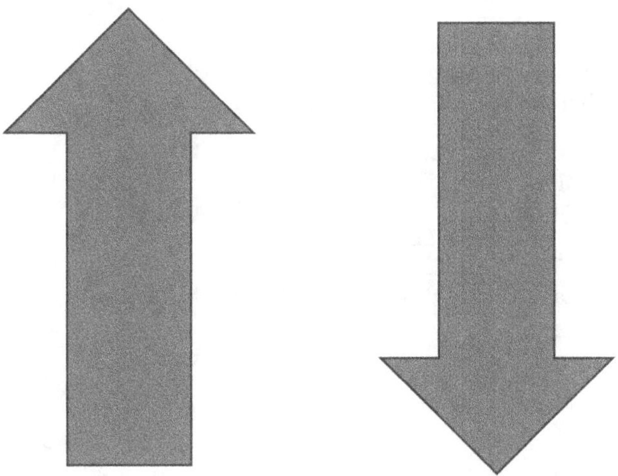

Flow Chart of Steps in Human Resource Recruitment and Selection Procedure (Abasolo, 1991)

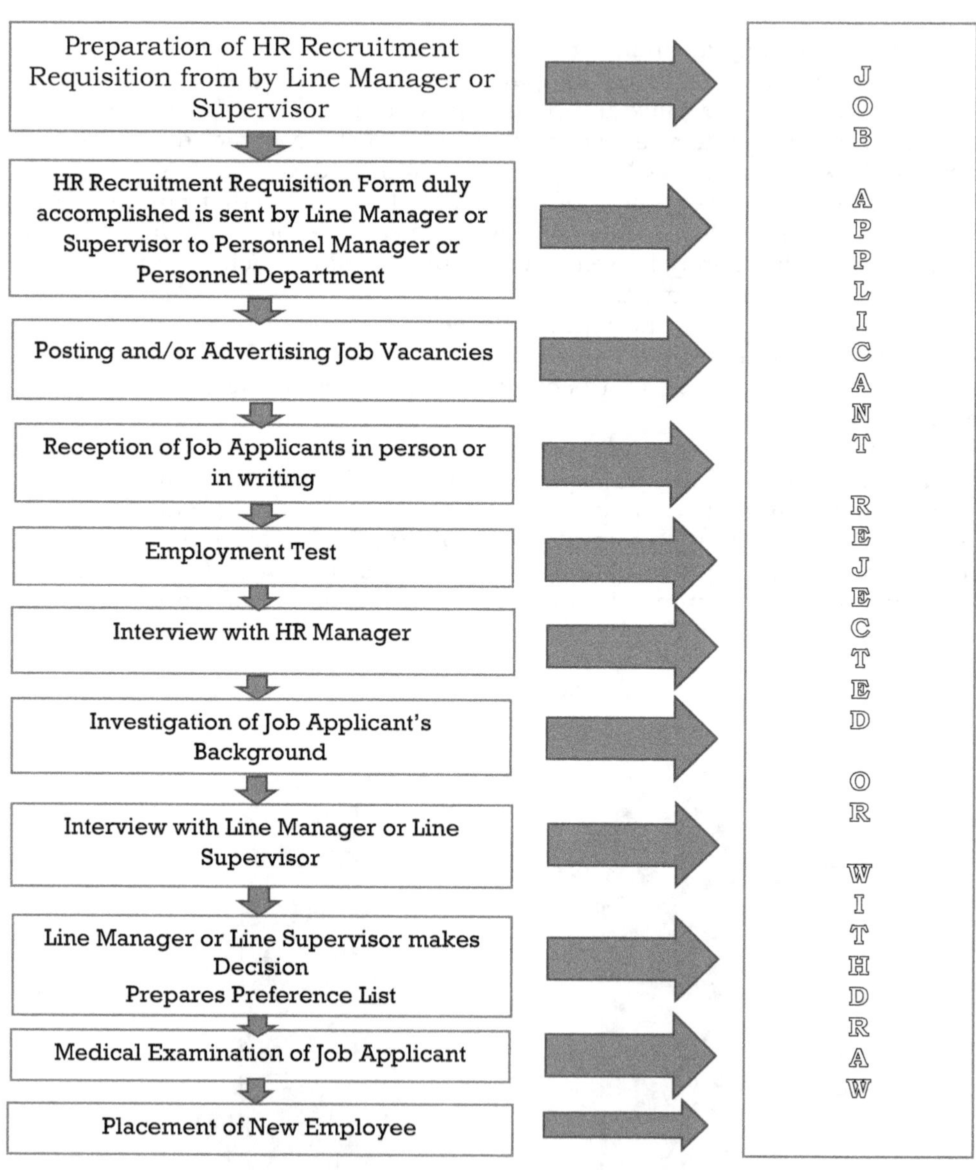

Appointment in the Armed Forces of the Philippines

Republic Act 291 and Executive Order 237 as implemented by Circular 1, General Headquarters, Armed Forces of the Philippines dated 09 July 1974 are the legal basis for applicants to qualify for appointment as officers of the armed forces. Under this circular, applicants shall be a natural born citizen of the Philippines, of good moral character, physically qualified under existing regulations for active military service, within the age bracket prescribed by law as follows – at least 21 years of age but not more than 26 on the date of appointment in the regular force for Philippine Army, Philippine Navy, and Philippine Air Force, except graduates of the Philippine Military Academy who will be appointed upon graduation from the academy. For the PMA Corps of Professors, age requirements must be at least 23 years of age but not more than 42 years old on the date of appointment (Ortigoza, 2010).

Executive Order 237 provides that applications for the Corps of Professors with bachelor's degree shall be appointed with a military-grade of captain and academic rank of assistant professor, an applicant with a master's degree shall be appointed with military-grade of Major and academic rank of associate professor, and an applicant with a doctorate shall be appointed with a military-grade of lieutenant colonel and academic rank of professor.

Executive Order 284 prescribes rules and regulations governing the administration of the civilian faculty of the Philippine Military Academy shall maintain and update its Faculty Merit System by policies and guidelines issued herein:

a. Recruitment. The applicant shall have the appropriate training and experience in the subject of the field of discipline he is applying for;

b. Selection. The applicant shall undergo a stringent selection process composed of two levels of interviews, teaching demonstration, physical and neuro-psychological examination, and background investigation before his or her appointment as member of the civilian faculty; and

c. Appointment. The PMA Superintendent shall initially appoint the applicant as a faculty member on a contractual basis to a faculty rank determined according to the criteria for evaluation used by state universities and colleges, higher education institutions, and technical education institutions. After one year of satisfactory service, such faculty members may be recommended for regular or permanent appointment.

Chapter III

DEVELOPMENT

After an employee has been selected and recruited, he or she must be developed to better fit the job and organization. Some degree of training and education should take Space as no one is a perfect fit at the time of hiring. The development would include both training to increase skill in performing a specific job and education to increase general knowledge and understanding of the total environment.

Planned development programs will return values to the organization in terms of increased productivity, heightened morale, reduced cost, and greater organizational stability and flexibility to adapt to changing external requirements. Such programs will also help meet the needs of individuals in their search for work assignments that can assist up to life-long careers.

According to Stahl (1983), training has been widely accepted as an integral part of management. However, most often than not, managers do not want to risk losing their staff members by training them for better things. They know that persons with advanced education have shorter careers and are more mobile as they seek an appropriate particular field of work.

Development Definition

Development refers to a learning experience for a longer duration. It is concerned with improving intellectual or mental capabilities in the performance of a given job or in preparation for assuming greater responsibilities as an employee moves upward organizational ladder (Abasolo, 1991).

Personnel Development – any attempt to improve current or future management performance by imparting knowledge, changing attitudes, or increasing skills (Dressler, 1991).

Career Development - refers to helping individuals plan their future careers within the organization to help them achieve maximum self-development and to help the organization achieve its objectives. It is helping people continue to grow and develop after they begin their employment. A career is a sequence of work-related experiences individuals acquire during the span of their work lives (Cherrington 1995).

Ideal Management Development Program as explained by Pacita Absolo:

The superior has responsibility for the development of his subordinates. He should determine on-the-job training needs, and control attendance at special or general courses. Most effectively, he would help the subordinate set performance goals, give him responsibility and make him accountable, and jointly appraise progress.

The manager has the opportunity to reflect on his role as a manager. This should occur early in his career and gain at changes in the managerial role, e.g., promotion to second-level manager, entrance to top management. He should be helped to review the precepts and practices of effective managers and to question his style of managing.

His superior and the manager development staff takes the initiative to establish and maintain a consulting relationship with him. The manager needs someone with whom to discuss problems. Other managers can help. Sometimes a consultant who is not involved can be of more help. Managers often do not seek assistance, or may not even know of its availability: therefore, others must take initiative.

The supervisor receives guidance in handling routine. At the time of his appointment, he would receive a handbook, much like some secretarial handbooks, which tell him how to handle routine matters such as completing time cards and making requisitions. It need not go into details of processing the work, a matter better left to the more efficient secretary. Rather than formal courses, a programmed instruction format may prove to be an excellent way for the superior to become familiar with these matters.

The manager has a thorough grounding in personnel policy. He must understand company policy and enough of the procedures and relevant laws to keep himself and the company out of trouble and to do a positive job of selling the company to the employees. He knows and feels that the personnel or industrial relations department exists to help him and can be called upon at any time.

The manager has the opportunity for training in the use of various management tools. These tools include engineering management procedure, PERT, and budgeting. When he will perform a marketing function, he learns to prepare proposals. This instruction consists of more than lectures. His superior continues the instruction by coaching him through the job. A possible, but less desirable, alternative would be to have experience in a simulated task. Every such experience, whether on a working team or in a management game, is reviewed to maximize the learning. A three-to- six-month assignment to a management-development staff can be extremely useful.

The manager has the responsibility and is accountable. Reality provided by accountability makes practice more effective. Since the manager holds the job for an indefinite period, he faces consequences and cannot plan an "end game" hoping the problem will go away. The boss also gives the man a frequent pat on the back and helps him to identify those things he did that resulted in good management.

The manager studies and reads widely in management and other professional fields. A manager should know the environment within which he works so that he can assess its impact upon his activities. His environment includes company operations, the business world, and the social and technical world. He should be able to adapt to new developments to his operation when they are relevant.

Periodic performance review sessions are held. In addition to the critiques of performance which should occur with the completion of specific tasks, sessions between the boss and his subordinate help both to take stock of their operation. These face-to-face discussions occur at least annually to answer this question, "How are we doing and how can we help each other to reach our individual and collective goals?"

The manager is helped to become a businessman, opportunities for education in business include how the customers and the company operate regarding contracts and pricing, administration of sub-contracts, computation of burden, etc. The theoretical aspect of these matters could be treated in a college course while the applications to the specific company and industry are dealt with in the job or an in-house course. A management game, played with a computer, can provide a model and help the manager to understand his world-provided the game is properly used.

The manager is helped to understand himself and others. The company provides a means to help the manager gain insight into human behavior. In some cases, behavior laboratories or sensitivity training would be appropriate.

Human Resources Development

The effective defense of our country rests on the quality of our regular fighting force and the citizen armed force. The focus of defense in human resource development is twofold: first, to be able to gain and maintain quality people and second, to enhance the professionalism of our corps of officers and the rank and file in the enlisted and civilian corps. The object of HRD is to be able to put the right soldier, sailor, or airman in the right job at the right time and place supported by a competent civilian workforce.

Objectives of HRD

First, the development of a highly professional and strategically minded defense and military leadership through a combination of education and training, professional assignments, and self-development programs.

Second, the enhancement of managerial and technological expertise particularly in the fields of research and development systems acquisition.

Third, the enhancement of our competence and merit-based personnel management systems particularly in promotion and assignment.
Fourth, the improvement of the soldier's "quality of life" through the provision of the basics health services and housing as well facilities that will provide a decent life for the soldier and his families like centers for learning, child care amenities, family support centers, recreation facilities, commissaries, in-camp transport amenities, and other beneficial programs and facilities.

Reserved Force for Development

Citizen-based defense calls for the development of a readily available reserve force that is well organized, well-trained, and properly equipped. The "total force concept" of mobilization of our national resources for defense must be strengthened through the sound integration of the Armed Forces and the Reserve Force. Like the regular force, the reserve must be properly led and managed in all aspects-personnel, training, supply, material, and financial.

The facilities and resources of the Armed Forces of the Philippines may not be enough to respond to national emergencies. In addition to the organization and maintenance of reserve forces, the guidance for future reserve force planning and programming is the establishment of a system to mobilize and integrate into the regular defense force the manpower and resources of the civilian community who are not part of reserve forces, particularly those in the business community, public utilities, non-governmental organizations, and local government units. Specific sectors targeted for mobilization in times of crisis include airlines, shipping lines, fishing industries, transport companies, and medical facilities.

Training and Development

Training and development are planned efforts to facilitate employee learning of job-related behaviors to improve employee performance. Sometimes, the term "training" is distinguished as the efforts to increase employee skills on present jobs while the term "development" refers to the efforts oriented toward improvements relevant to future jobs (Bartol, 1991). Training is further defined as instructions which emphasize job-specific and near transfer learning objective. Traditionally, it is a skill-based instruction, as opposed to education (Piskurich, 1993).

According to Stahl (1983), the necessity to conduct training could be for various reasons. To mention a few: people are recruited not for specific job but for broad categories which are scattered throughout the organization; thus, they require orientation in the work of the unit; the quickest way to adjust to organizational change is through deliberate orderly training fit employees; the specific skills required of a job are seldom acquired in general institution; training is the process through which specialist can keep abreast of their specialty as occupational fields usually evolve; it is more efficient to improve the skill of existing employees to an optimum level than to rely upon initial recruitment of a highly skilled person; an orderly study of policies and programs of an organization enhances cohesiveness and coordination and builds mutual respect and confidence; films, talks, interesting reading materials, seminars, planned staff conferences, or other training devices creates enthusiasm for the work than does leading by trial and error; and training accounts the difference between organizations in qualities such as knowledge of employees about their own job as well as their total organization, courtesy and attitude towards the public, interest in the work, and skill and speed in performing a service.

Training Purposes

Induction and Orientation - new employees are introduced to the organization, to their segment of work, and to the conditions of employment that will affect them and their future.

Performance Improvement - Sometimes referred to as "refresher courses", the intention is to keep employees up to date in their respective fields of activity.

Broadening Staff Usefulness - Has a similar objective to performance improvement but is more complex as it aims to extend and expand the horizons and utility of staff members. It may mean an improvement of supervision or preparation for greater responsibility.

Developing Top Leadership - Training of executives at the highest rung of the hierarchy.

Types of Training Programs

Orientation - is a formal program designed to provide the new employee with information about the company and their jobs.

Technical Skills Training - is oriented toward providing specialized knowledge and developing facility in the use of methods, processes, and techniques associated with a particular trade.

Management Development Programs - focus on developing managerial s l Is for use at the supervisory managerial, and executive levels.

Phases of Training

In their book, Management, Bartol, and Martin explain that training efforts generally encompass three main phases: the assessment phase, the training design and implementation phase, and the evaluation phase.

The assessment phase involves identifying training needs, setting training objectives, and developing criteria against which to evaluate the results of the training program. Within the assessment phase, training requirements are determined by conducting a "need analysis". A Needs Analysis is an assessment of an organization's training needs that is developed by considering overall organizational requirements, tasks (identified through job analysis) associated with jobs for which training is needed, and the degree to which individuals can perform those tasks effectively.

The training design and implementation phase involve determining training methods, developing training materials, and conducting the training. Within this phase are several training methods that can be used, which can be categorized into three: Information presentation methods that entail teaching facts skills, attitudes, or concepts without expecting trainees to put what they learn into practice during the training. Examples are lectures, reading lists, videotapes, and most computerized instructions; Simulation training methods involve providing artificial situations that offer trainees a means of practicing their learning during training. Examples include case analysis and role-playing. On-the-job training (OJT) methods focus on having the trainee learn while performing a job, usually with the help of a knowledgeable trainer. Examples include job rotation, vestibule training (in which the trainee learns in a separate area that is set up to approximate as closely as possible the actual job situation), and on-the-job coaching (in which the trainee performs the job under the direct guidance of a trainer).

The evaluation phase entails assessing the results of the training against the criteria developed during the assessment phase. Major ways to evaluate framing include measuring participants' reactions to the training to determine how useful they thought it was assessing actual learning (perhaps through the test before and after the training), determining the extent of behavioral change, and measuring actual results on the job (such as increased output).

Training Techniques

Orientation Training - Usually precedes the beginning of any productive work experience Its content includes such diverse topics as the history of the organization, company policies and procedures, employee benefits, career paths available a tour of facilities, a review of resources, and major organizational philosophies and programs.

Vestibule Training - used almost exclusively for skill development, vestibule programs involve setting up realistic production — like equipment and materials away from the actual workplace. Many of the learning principles are incorporated (participation, practice, feedback) and the assessment of skills developed is readily observable or measurable. The time required is flexible, depending on the learner's pace of development and the job's complexity. The cost of development and operation may both be high and prohibitive for the small firm. This training is most appropriate for those positions requiring the use of mechanical equipment.

Films - used to demonstrate appropriate supervisory behaviors, to communicate the essential elements of a procedure, or event to convince the viewers to change their perspective on a given issue.

Videotape - closely aligned with films. Available in black and white, color playback, with sound. Most effective when applied to such individual trainees (as in the development of personal selling skills) and less effective as simply a group demonstration device.

Lecture - singularly useful for transmitting knowledge and impractical for attitude change or skill development. Widely used, economical to develop, flexible in application both about time and group size and its effectiveness can be readily assessed by objective tests of knowledge. It incorporates very little of the concept of trainee involvement.

Program Instruction - this has required increasing popularity. Oriented primarily toward knowledge acquisition. PI most clearly (of all techniques discussed) incorporates the major principles of learning. Its highlights are self-pacing, individualized entry at the appropriate background level, immediate feedback, correction and reinforcement, active involvement of the trainee, and arrangement of the material in ascending order of complexity. PI requires minimal trainee supervision, but it is time - consuming to properly prepare materials, PI texts can be used with almost any size group A PI program is inexpensive to administer, although relatively costly to develop.

Correspondence – this method involves the receipt of inputs (text manuals, instructional guides) and requires the student to absorb the material and usually submit a completed examination before the subsequent phases of the material.

Training costs are fixed (the cost of the course is known in advance). Supervision required is minimal or absent, and any number of trainees can be simultaneously handled. Trainee participation, self-pacing, and feedback are incorporated. The most serious weakness is probably the difficulty (time-lag) in obtaining answers to student questions. The student can become extremely frustrated at the lack of on the spot supportive feedback and redirection when needed.

On the Job Techniques

Techniques that allow the worker to produce a product or provide service simultaneously as the training takes place:

Apprenticeship - combine the features of the on-the-job and off-the-job techniques. New workers are provided with a balance of the theoretical and practical through both instruction and experience. The learning principles highlighted are participation, a logical progression from step to step, feedback, the use of multiple senses, and adequate practice time. The administrative cost of apprenticeship programs is the length of the program, the proportion of the classroom hours, the number of individuals enrolled, and the expected level of productivity of the trainees while they are working. The training staff includes trained workers in the occupation who supervise the trainees while they work. This can be a strength or weakness of the program, depending upon the technical knowledge and ability of these trained workers to effectively develop subordinate workers.

Job Instruction (JIT) - method of training trainers to train workers. The prerequisites are the evaluation of the trainees before instruction, throughout job analysis to determine the important components and detailed schedule of instruction. The cost of JIT can be substantial in terms of both the analysis required and the high ratio of trainers to trainees in the early phases. Time usage is quite efficient, however, since the trainee can gauge the progress of the trainee through direct observation. Skill development is the primary objective. Learning principles involved are feedback, correct sequencing of tasks, practice time, communication of learning objectives, and the opportunity for reinforcement of appropriate behavior.

Job Rotation - this technique involves the systematic movement of an individual from one job to another after sufficient time intervals to allow for basic competency (if not proficiency) in each succeeding job. The purpose is to acquaint the employee with the nature of, and the interrelationship between, each of several jobs. This can have motivational effects in terms of developing the trainees' skills in several areas (job enlargement). It has a beneficial effect on the organization in that it produces back up employees who can be called upon when other employees are ill, on vacation, are terminated, or when extra workload demands arise.

The primary expense factor is the relative inefficiency low productivity, disruption of workflow, possible safety threat) of the workers as they become acclimated to the new position.

Job Relations Program is almost endless. Job Relations Programs seldom fit neatly into a format of planned progression from simple to complex. Also, the limited amount of time spent in each position virtually precludes the opportunity to practice newly acquired skills adequately. In job relation, the factors of feedback, active participation, and opportunity for reinforcement may be present.

Coaching - involves the formal pairing of a skilled person with an unskilled trainee, and making the coach responsible for the trainee's skill development. This has the merit of being inexpensive from a direct cost standpoint. It is highly personalized from a standpoint of teacher-student ratio (often 1:1) and requires no special equipment or facilities similar to job rotation in its multiple objectives of skill, knowledge, and attitude development.

Coaching incorporates the use of multiple senses, makes it easier to gauge the trainee's desire to learn (because of the extensive degree of coach-trainee contact, and provides an opportunity for feedback, reinforcement, involvement, and practice. The single biggest drawback is the difficulty of discovering or developing persons with effective coaching skills who can not only demonstrate but also explain why they work as they do.

Administration of Training

Stahl (1983) cited that there are three key players in the administration of training: the training specialist, instructors, and the evaluation system.

Training Specialist. The training specialist has the role of an advisor and coordinator. He must also be a stimulator, a provocateur, and an evaluator. He sometimes functions as an instructor, but usually, he leads in joint efforts with management to design a program, secure appropriate instructors and conference leaders, and to see the formal courses are operated effectively and efficiently. He must possess a keen insight into human behavior and a full grasp of the mission of his agency.

Instructors. One of the difficult steps in developing a group-training program is the selection and preparation of those who are expected to help instruct others. The training officer must be acquainted with the resources available. He must be relentless but skillful in training the trainer. He must know how to speak before a group and to elicit discussion, must master his subject matter, and must be able to employ modem learning aids and techniques that are relevant to his subject.

Evaluation. The most underdeveloped aspect of training is its evaluation. Some may despair at evaluating training effort because they seek precision and certainty. We can only, however, approximate the quality of training results. But this should not stop the effort as there are at least quasi-scientific methods that help determine the extent to which a particular program is effective.

Education and Training

Proper education and training are the keys to professionalism and force preparedness. High-quality education and training programs result in good officers, soldiers, sailors, airmen, and civilian personnel. This is turn translates to a quality force.

Education and training remain a top priority in defense activities. Schools and training institutions must be properly supported in terms of qualified and competent instructors and trainers, information sources (library, internet, publications), and administrative support. Education programs must be designed to promote intellectual integrity and self-development.

Domestic and foreign schooling programs must be reviewed to make them congruent to the training needs of the Armed Forces and responsive to the AFP's changing operational environment. Educational opportunities arising out of defense arrangements with other countries will be fully harnessed. In managing training programs, the AFP must be able to match assignments with training performance and give the individual the training necessary to effectively perform in the job. The selection criteria for both domestic and foreign schooling should not only be rank and position but more importantly, competence and service potential.

It must be emphasized that foreign education and training is not a substitute for local training but a compliment. Our objective is to develop a truly indigenous education and training program for our soldiers and civilian personnel.

Armed Forces Education and Training

At the strategic level, a sound and appropriate program for continuing education and scientific inquiry for national defense, in both formal and non-formal contexts, needs to be institutionalized. An important component of this would be the education of defense and military personnel in sound resource management and policy formulation. As necessary and as resources would allow, "think tanks" will be established at appropriate levels of the Defense Department and the Armed Forces of the Philippines to conduct scientific policy analysis and management studies on defense and security questions. Defense research and development, especially in key fields of national defense such as information technology, communications electronics, navigation systems, weapons technology, and logistical and material systems, like science and medicine will be strengthened.

The Defense Department will undertake steps toward a world-class, professional continuing education program, particularly in the higher centers of defense learning at the National Defense College of the Philippines and the AFP Joint Command and Staff College. DND will see to it that the strategic levels of learning are harmonized with the operational and tactical levels. Like other facets of the defense organization, the continuing education and training program requires regular and systematic monitoring and evaluation. They should be subjected to intensive curriculum review to ensure that they are consistent with the doctrine and national defense policy.

The PMA and the service OCS to include technical schools are the institutions where officers' military education begins. It is here where the cadets are developed so that by the time, they graduate they shall possess the character, the broad and basic military skills and education, essential for a successful pursuit of a progressive military career. A Code of ideals and core values are taught and cultivated during these training phases.

Professional Military Education

After commission, the skills training of the officer continues with technical training such as basic infantry training, basic flight training, naval officer's qualification course, etc. They are taught in technical training schools. Throughout his career, he continues with his professional military education with studies such as the Advanced Officers Course, Command and Staff Course, Joint Services and Command Staff Course, and the Master in National Security Administration.

One of the missions of the AFP related to the development of military professionals is to determine the correct content of professional military education courses and other relevant programs to educate its personnel This is done so at different levels in the organization and by different military schools. The right curricula and training are studied and determined by the different Academic Boards of these schools^ The General Headquarters, through its Education and Training Staff (J-8), reviews and approves these proposals.

The service also offers equal opportunities for its members of all ranks and specialties to develop their potentials. Facilities for self-improvement such as off-duty education, technical training, OJT Programs, and Career Development Courses are made available to all individuals. Each officer is encouraged to give himself the benefit of every opportunity to increase his technical qualifications and enhance his professional and military knowledge. However, only the best qualified and most deserving can be assured of promotion and be guaranteed a progressive military career.

Armed Forces Training Objectives and Tasks

The broad objectives are to provide adequate individual training opportunities for military personnel to acquire knowledge and skills to efficiently perform duties, to attain teamwork proficiency from unit training activities to prepare AFP units to carry out assigned missions satisfactorily, to enhance the development of a higher degree of coordination and nitty of purpose in actual AFP military campaigns through an improved and standardized training in practical concepts and procedures of joint (ground, land, air, and naval) operations, to optimize the training of a reserve force through a revitalized CMT (including WATC and CAT) programs, 20-year old training system, a reservists re-training responsive to the programmed fill-up of the standing force and consistent with mobilization objectives of the AFP, to strengthen the para-military capability and self-sufficiency of small communities and other public-private agencies concerned with peace and order through effective and viable CAFGU and related training programs, and to upgrade the educational attainment and outlook of AFP personnel by means of an expanded scholarship attendance in more productive seminars or other management and professional development courses.

Military Training Objectives

The armed forces training mission and its supporting tasks can only be accomplished if the following eight (8) basic objectives of military training are achieved.

Military Discipline. All soldiers must recognize and respect authority and give unhesitating obedience to that authority. Training in military discipline is continuous. Its principles are applied in every military activity and every military activity reinforces the principles.

Health, Strength, and Endurance. This objective is essential if soldiers are to withstand the rigors and hardships of combat. Armed Forces composed of men possessing these physical characteristics and military discipline has the foundation for becoming an unconquerable force.

Technical Proficiency. Each individual must possess sufficient knowledge and achieve the skills necessary to properly perform his assigned duties. He must know all aspects of his job thoroughly. He must also be able to use and maintain the weapons, equipment, material available in support of the mission.

Teamwork Each individual must be taught to employ his technical proficiency with other team members and to operate as a part of that team. He must subordinate his interest to those of the team as a whole.

Tactical Proficiency. This is the ultimate goal of military training and a culmination of all the other objectives. The unit can operate effectively in combat to accomplish the mission stated in its table of organization and equipment.

Leadership. A leader must be qualified professionally and possesses personal qualities that will inspire confidence and loyalty and confidence in subordinates. Some of the personal characteristics necessary are courage, mental and physical stability, and energy, and a sense of justice. The development of leadership is a primary consideration in the training of all officers and non-commissioned officers.

Morale and Esprit de Corps. Morale and esprit de corps refer to the mental state of troops - their confidence, courage, zeal, and pride in their organization. In peacetime, it is the measure of their contentment and well-being; in wartime, it is the measure of their will to do and the courage to execute unhesitatingly the arduous task assigned them. Individual morale and esprit de corps denote optimism and confidence; both stimulated determination and physical effort. Strength in members, equipment, and material resources cannot wholly compensate for lack of morale within a unit. Morale and esprit de corps are influenced by many factors, but primarily by good leadership, thorough comprehensive training, and the pride and confidence of the individual in himself and his unit.

Initiative and Adaptability. The energy and ability to initiate action promptly to meet any situation are essential qualities for every individual member of a military force. The mission of any unit is accomplished by the prompt and, when necessary, independent action of individuals and small groups. Therefore, the development of initiative and adaptability is a very important factor to be attained in training. These objectives are developed effectively through practice in occupying positions or responsibility and by training that frequently requires the individual to rely on his resources.

Basic Concepts of Training

The following basic concepts of training will govern all types of AFP Training Management Program: the dignity of the individual undergoing training is not violated, given proper leadership and training, the average man can become an effective soldier, the applicatory system of training must effectively meet the needs of training, training progresses from basic to advanced subjects and from individual to unit training, skills are acquired through supervised practice, doctrines and techniques are standard throughout the command, and the commander is responsible for training his unit.

Relationship Between the Trainer and The Training Manager

Training Manager. Training managers are responsible for the planning, organization, conduct, and evaluation of training. Training managers include the commanders who develop a training program or who provide training guidance to another commander. Under present Army policies (AR 350-1), battalion commanders and separate company commanders are the principal training managers. However, company commanders and the operations/training officers of commands developing training programs also employ limited resources (human, physical, financial, and time) in a manner that permits efficient and effective development of individuals and units so they can accomplish their peacetime and wartime missions.

Trainers. Trainers are those whose duties include the requirement to prepare, conduct, and evaluate training (e.g. and infantry platoon sergeant who prepares, conducts, and evaluates mortar training for his fellow NCOs in the company). Although the process that both the trainer and the training manager use to meet their responsibilities appear quite similar, it differs significantly in practice. Whereas the training manager establishes or selects the training objectives which are critical to the accomplishment of his mission, the trainer is responsible for accomplishing one or more of these objectives. Therefore, the trainer's scope is narrower, more concentrated, and more exciting.

Training Structure

The training being conducted by active reserve component units of the AFP at any given period can be appropriately placed into one of the three major categories: individual training, unit training, and combined training. These categories have been established for convenience in planning and to indicate definite stages of progress. These categories may be further subdivided into phases of training, depending largely upon the type of organization, its assigned mission, and the existing state of training.

Individual training is a broad term that applies to the training received by an individual without regard to grade or level of proficiency. It applies to the training of recruits as replacements for units in training or combat. It applies to the schooling and training of officers, noncommissioned officers, and specialists. Individual training begins when the individual enters the military service and continues throughout his service. Initially, the emphasis is placed on the development of the individual as a basic soldier. Then, the emphasis is shifted to the development of his primary skill to perform a duty assignment within a unit.

Unit training emphasizes the training of individuals to function as members of a team or unit. It integrates the smaller units into coordinated battlefield teams within their respective branches. These units develop their tactical proficiency, perfect operating procedures, and the use of weapons, manpower, and equipment. Unit training continues to emphasize individual training by providing the opportunity for soldiers trained in individual skills to practice these skills and to learn the value of teamwork. Advanced individual training is continued for those specialists requiring additional training during the development of unit proficiency.

Combined training develops combine arms teams composed of branches that normally conduct combined combat operations. This type of training is generally initiated in the early stages of unit training. It continues as a major area of emphasis throughout the development of units, from platoon through division level (advanced stages in the combined training of units may include joint training exercises that develop effective teams of combined services to insure the balanced forces necessary for major operations).

Subject

The subject areas in military training can be groups into three: basic subject, technical training, and tactical training.

Basic Subjects. By nature, and content, these subjects are directed toward developing military discipline in individuals and within units. Dismounted drill, military courtesy, interior guard duty, physical training, marches, and battle drill are an example of these subjects.

Technical Training. This includes those subject areas designed to develop the technical ability of the individual to perform his technical function. Technical training of the individual includes those subjects designed to teach the fundamental of his duty assignments, such as weapon training, marksmanship, communications, or clerical training. Technical training of the unit depends largely on the organization, mission, and branch of the unit but it generally includes fundamental subjects designed to support its tactical performance.

Tactical Training. This includes those subjects and exercises conducted to train the individual in his role and to develop the proficiency of the unit to accomplish the mission for which it was organized. Effectiveness in tactical training depends to a large extent on the effectiveness of the disciplinary and technical training previously conducted and on the degree of realism achieved in the training exercises. This training may be conducted in field or garrison training areas using the applicatory exercise.

Individual Training

Individual training is a continuous process that begins the moment a man enters the military service and does not terminate until he leaves. It continues throughout his career, both in schools and units, or other organizations. It is the source of production of proficient units and combined arms teams. Individual skills must be periodically reviewed throughout a soldier's span of service and each degree of complexity in the development of the individual continues until he leaves the service, or reaches the limit of his ability. The knowledge and skills which the soldier has mastered must be periodically practiced and refreshed so that they can be retained.

Initially, individual training familiarizes the new soldier with his surroundings and acquaints him with his responsibilities as a soldier. During the period, he receives short orientations on what is expected of him during his service and what he may expect from the military service. The objective of the commander responsible for the initial conduct of individual training is to bring about a rapid transition from civilian to soldier status. Practice, drills, and physical training develop knowledge, discipline, coordination, and teamwork in execution. The primary purpose of this training is to instill in each precise and orderly habits. As the soldier progresses, he develops proficiency in weapons familiarization and marksmanship, a firm foundation in the fundamentals of basic military subjects. His training is directed toward the development of skills concerning job performance. Application in later phases of training ensures a high degree of proficiency.

Replacement Training

Replacement training is the training conducted to provide new soldiers with basic military knowledge. It develops their proficiency for a specific duty assignment within a unit or organization. The AFP assists in maintaining the operational proficiency of units of the major service commands by providing qualified basic soldiers and specialists as replacements for unit personnel losses, and in some cases, as fillers for newly activated units. These individuals are normally trained in training centers, special service schools, and in designated TOE units of the major service commands within the country. The qualified replacement must be properly disciplined, physically conditioned, technically qualified, and emotionally prepared to perform successfully in combat operations. This training provides a continuous flow of qualified basic soldiers, as individuals or in packets of variable size to units in combat or conducting peacetime training requirements.

The replacement training phase consists of the basic combat and advanced individual training phases. The AFP has established mandatory training requirements in time and subject areas to ensure standardization of training and qualification to replacements for the major service commands. These requirements are also contained in applicable training programs of the major service commands which cover all replacement training in consonance with current AFP standards.

Basic Combat Training. This phase of training transforms the civilian into a basic soldier. The basic combat training phase is prescribed in AFP Training Programs. The objective of basic combat training is to develop a disciplined, highly motivated soldier who is qualified in his basic weapon, physically conditioned, and drilled in the fundamentals of soldiery. The emphasis during this phase is on motivation, proficiency in the use of individual weapons, disciplinary training, and physical fitness.

Advanced Individual Training. Advanced individual training is the second stage of individual training and completes the mandatory replacement training. The objective of the advanced individual training is to qualify an individual to perform the job required by a TOE or table of distribution (TD) assignment. This phase of training may be conducted in training centers, service schools, or in TOE units; it may be accomplished by on the job training (OJT), schooling or a combination of these. Upon successful completion of training in this phase, individuals are awarded the military occupation or technical specialty (MOS/AFS) for which they were trained.

After the completion of replacement training, any individual found to be deficient in his primary MOS/AFS is retrained until he reaches proper proficiency level, retraining is impractical, appropriate personnel procedures are undertaken to assign him a new primary MOS/AFS that is commensurate with his demonstrated capabilities and qualifications.

Development of Training Program

Every training manager follows some methods when he develops a training program. He analyzes the unit's mission, available training resources, and current training status to determine both individual and unit training objectives. Unfortunately, most training managers soon find themselves wanting to conduct more training than the unit's limited training resources.

These limited resources - human, physical, financial, and time - force the manager to choose between what he wants to do and what he can do. Resource limitations compel him to concentrate on the training most beneficial to his unit's assigned missions. Eventually, the training manager must evaluate completed training to determine the degree to which has original objectives have been met.

Career Professional Education for AFP Officers

Career Professional Course	Sponsor	Duration	Subjects
Master in National Security Administration (MNSA)	National Defense College of the Philippines (NDCP)	12 months	Formulation of National Security, Research Methodology, Policy Science, Socio-Cultural, International System and Foreign Policy,

			Political System, Economics of National Security, Management of National Security Studies, National Security Exercise.
Joint Service Command and Staff Course (JSCSC)	AFP Joint Services Command and Staff College (AFPJSCSC)	8 months	Introductory Study, Warfare Study, Resource Management Conflict Studies, Joint / Combined Operations, Political Warfare, Capstone CPX, and Enhancement Program
Command and General Staff Course	Philippine Army (PA) Training and Doctrines Command (TRADOC)	7 months	PA Introductory Studies, General and Staff Management Strategic Conflict Studies, Military Operations, Professional Enhancement Program
	Philippine Air Force (PAF) Air Command and Staff College (ACGSC)	6 months	Environmental Studies, Air Operations Command, Leadership and Management Studies
	Philippine Navy (PN) Naval Education and Training Command (NETC)	4 months	Command Management and Administrative Strategic Studies, Naval / Maritime Operations Integration
Advance Courses	PA TRADOC	4 months	PA Map Reading II, Communication Skills LIC Operations, AFPOS Subjects
	PAF ACSC	6 months	PAF Communication Skills, Leadership and Management, Command and Staff Function, Environmental Studies, AFP Operations

	PN NETC	7 months	PN Communication Skills, Naval Command and Staff, Military Management, Military Operations, Staff Study / Research
Basic Courses	PA TRADOC	4 months	PA Map Reading I, LIC Operations, Introduction to Conventional Warfare, Value Formation, AFPOS Subjects.
	PAF ACSC	6 months	PAF Communication Skills, Development, Leadership and Management, Command and Staff Functions
	PN NETC	7 months	PN Orientations, Communication Skills, Sea Phase, Naval Management, Deck and Gunnery, Naval Operations Navigation, OJT.

Suggestion Programs

Suggestion programs are formal programs that askes employees to write down or otherwise express any suggestions they have to improve work methods or any other aspect of their job. A response rate in a suggestion program is typically about 15 percent, of which about one-quarter of the responses are implemented. Suggestion programs very often revolve around topics such as how to save money in an area or how to reduce accidents (Drummond,1990).

Suggestion Box

The suggestion box allows employees to make written suggestions to certain problems. Some operators purposely set up management-employee meetings to allow employees to ask questions and make comments, positive and negative, about anything going on within the organization.

Communication in HRM

Communication is the process of transmitting information from one person to another (Griffin, 1996). Communication involves the transfer of meaning. If no information or ideas have been conveyed, communication has not taken place. The speaker who is not heard or the writer who is not read does not communicate (Robbins, 1988). Communication needs a sender, message, receiver, and feedback.

In her book, "Human Resources Management for the Hospitality Industry," Karen Drummond explains the communication process:

The communication process is a sequence of steps involving a sender, a message, and a receiver. The sender forms an idea, puts it into words, and then transmit it. During this process, the way the sender gets the message across depends greatly on the person's attitude, perceptions, communication skills, and goal, as well as the method used in sending it. The sender essentially has the responsibility of transmitting a clear and creating understanding during this process.

Feedback in the communication process is very important to make sure the receiver understands the message. Drummond explains that messages are conveyed using symbols such as words – either spoken or written – and non-verbal communication – independent of words – in the case of spoken messages.

Upward, Downward, and Lateral Communication

Upward communication includes the suggestion box, employee satisfaction survey, open-door policy, management-employee meeting, and exit interviews. Downward communication involves policies and procedures, job descriptions, performance evaluations, training, and the like; it is mostly of an informative or directive nature. Communication between superiors and subordinates is a downward communication. Within many organizations, goals, and objectives, policies, and so forth come from top management and are communicated downward, perhaps to the lowest-level employee. Downward communication helps to link the different levels of the organization together and to initiate the feedback process. Examples include employee meetings, employee handbooks, bulletin boards, company newsletters, feedback, coaching, and counseling. Lateral communication is among people at approximately the same level in the organization. employees need to meet social needs and coordinate their activities (Drummond, 1990).

Formal and Informal Communication

Formal communications refer to those that follow the authority chain of command or are part of the communications required to do one's job. When a boss requests a subordinate, he or she is communicating formally. So does the employee who takes a problem to his or her superior. Formal communication also occurs when two shipping clerks must interact to coordinate the customer's order.

Informal communications arise to meet employee needs. These communications are not approved by management, and there is no predetermined structural hierarchy by which they are defined. However, the lack of management sanction does not mean that informal communications do not exist. Employees form friendships, and cliques develop. These in turn allow employees to fill communication gaps within the formal channels. The informal communication system, therefore, serves two purposes. It permits employees to satisfy their need for social interaction. It can also improve an organization's performance by creating alternative, and frequently faster and more efficient, channels through which to communicate. A phone call to a friend in another department may ger an answer to a question in five minutes. Getting that same information through formal channels might require three levels of management and several days. Thus, informal communication can act as a support system for the formal channels (Robbins, 1988).

Performance Appraisal

A major HRM activity to improve corporate effectiveness and to realize employee productivity and efficiency is the performance appraisal. It takes place whether there are formal procedures for its conduct or not. It can have important ramifications at work where decisions that may affect career development and economic well-being are made based on the appraisal of one person by others.

In many organizations, two evaluation systems may be in use, the formal and the informal. The informal system is based on the presumptions of superiors on how well their subordinates are doing. Political and interpersonal processes influence it. Personnel who are liked better than others have an edge. On the other hand, the formal system is created by the organization to regularly and systematically measure employee performance (Ivancevich, 1995).

An organization's reward system is its most basic tool for managing employee motivation. An organizational reward system is the formal and informal mechanisms by which employee performance is defined, evaluated, and rewarded (Griffin, 1996).

Because of the drawbacks in using seniority as the sole promotion criterion, many organizations strongly consider current performance when promoting to the job of increased responsibility, especially in management and professional jobs. Seniority is given little or no weight in such cases. Instead, a candidate's performance appraisals, training and development history, formal education, special awards, and other performance data are often considered with an informal judgment of the employee's chances for success in a higher-level job. Using this approach, the chances that the organization will make an effective promotion decision are relatively good when both the candidate's present job and the higher job require similar skills and abilities.

Definition of Performance Appraisal

Performance appraisal is defined as the method by which the individual worker's efficiency in performing his duties and responsibilities in a given period is evaluated based on predetermined standards mutually set by the employee and his supervisor (Sison, 1991).

Performance Appraisal is known by many terms such as performance rating, efficiency rating, employee evaluation, service training, personnel rating, review of performance, and employee appraisal.

Reasons for Appraisal

There are several reasons why companies appraise their employees. These are (Clark, 1992):

To mold employee behavior according to company determined norms. Appraisal systems identify and reward behavior that conforms to the organization's beliefs and punishes those that does not. It can be used to counsel and discipline an employee to improve himself.

To enhance the consistency between employee actions and corporate goals. It brings corporate objectives to the attention of the employee relative to his contribution to achieving these goals. It can diagnose weak points as well as the strong points that the employee may not be aware of.

To improve the quality of human resource planning, in particular, training and succession. Training needs may be identified as well as the person who may be promoted.

To improve the quality of salary reviews. If salary decisions are related to performance, employees tend to perceive it as arbitrary.

To provide a record in cases of dismissal, demotions, grievances, or appeals. In a society where increased legislation and regulations concerning victimization, discrimination, and unfair dismissal, performance appraisal could be used as evidentiary support to justify the action of employers, research, and evaluation.

Appraisal data could be used to determine whether the various HR programs are effective. It can be used to validate selection tools such as a testing program, in communications - the evaluation is a basis for an on-going discussion between superior and subordinate about job-related matters. Through interaction, the parties get to know each other better and to improve supervision by making supervisors more aware of his duties.

Officer Evaluation Report

The Officer Evaluation Report is designed to provide the AFP with information on an officer's effectiveness and value which, together with other available data, can be used as a guide in personnel actions.

Purpose:

The purpose of the Evaluation Report is to rate each officer for every period of active service except while on leave before retirement, thus providing a basis of comparison among officers to:

1. Provide a measure of an officer's value to the service to be used as one of the bases for such personnel actions as promotion and separation.
2. Have officers utilized to best advantage by correct training, classification, and assignment?

On whom rendered and forms to be used:

1. Evaluation Reports will be rendered on each regular and reserve officer of all grades, except General/Flag Officers, in the active service.

2. On Officer-student at local military schools, Evaluation Reports will be made in AFP AGO 67-S in two (2) copies.
3. On Officer-students at foreign military schools, Evaluations, Evaluation from the head of the institution will be requested by TAG, AFP, in AFP AGO Form 67-S in two (2) copies.
4. On Officer- students at local or foreign civilian schools, Evaluation Reports from the head of the institution will be requested by TAG, APF, in AFP AGO Form 67- U in two (2) copies.
5. On Officer on duty outside the AFP or who are serving immediately under non-AFP Officials, Evaluation Reports will be requested by TAG, AFP, from the head of the office, organization, or agency in AFP AGO Form 67-C in two (2) copies.
6. On all other officers, reports will be made in AFP AGO Form 67-M in two (2) copies.

Whom rendered

The evaluation report will be rendered by a rater and an endorser. The rater is the immediate superior and is responsible for the immediate supervision, under the pertinent chain of command or start structure, of the rated officer (the officer on whom the report is submitted). The endorser is the immediate superior and is responsible for the immediate supervision, under the pertinent chain of command or staff structure, of the rater. Officers on detail with military or civilian schools, local or foreign, or on detail with civilian agencies, will be rated on Evaluation Reports by the designated reporting officers of such schools or agencies.

When Rendered

Periodic - It will be rendered for periods ending on dates as follows:

Grade and its equivalent in the PN	Period Ending
Lieutenants	31 January
Captains	20 February
Major and above	20 March

Relief of rater - It will be rendered upon relief of the rated officer from his primary duty assignment in a military unit or a civilian agency or when the rated officer is placed on TDY or DS in another unit for more than 30 days as specified by orders.

On special occasions as follows:

1. On completion of AADT, duty as a student (local or foreign) duty outside the AFP.
2. When, in the opinion of the rater, an individual is inability or performance of duty as to require reassignment, adverse personnel action, or disciplinary action.

3. When, in the opinion of the rater, the manner of performance of duty is so outstanding as to justify the submission of special reports.
4. In instances where the immediate superior (rater) dies or is missing, and more than thirty (30) days has elapsed since the rendition of the last report, reports will be rendered as of the date of the incident on all personnel normally rated by such individual by the officer who would have been the endorser.

General Instructions

Evaluation Reports are of such far-reaching importance to the AFP and to the individual officer such that the greatest care must be exercised in their preparation. Close attention to instructions contained in the form and to those in this Circular is mandatory to ensure proper completion. All unit commanders must take appropriate steps to ensure that all officers under them will be able to read and understand the contents of this Circular. All commanders will require officers under them to sign a certificate, which will be included in the MPF, that they have read and understood the contents of this Circular, within one month from the effective date of publication or within one month after an officer's call to active service.

Disciplinary action will be taken by the appropriate commanders of major services (action office - OTAG, GHQ in case of JAGS, MC, DS, CHS, MAC, Corps of Professors, WAC, NC, VC, and DCL officers assigned in GHQ) against officers concerned who fail to accomplish reports by this Circular. Report of disciplinary action taken will be transmitted to TAG, AFP.

All Officers should be impartial, accurate, objective, and judicious in rendering Evaluation Reports and should realize the serious necessity of a realistic officer evaluation in the AFP. Reporting Officers should not let close personal associations, animosities, prejudices, and biases influence them. Giving a rating higher than that merited by job performance is unfair not only to other officers but to the individual himself. Overall rating an officer may read to the assignment of duties for which he is not qualified. The idea, therefore, is to give ratings that are neither higher nor lower than merited.

The Evaluation Report is not to be used by superiors as a tool in counseling subordinates toward improved performance of duty. Raters shall instead continually correct deficiencies and stimulate improvement among subordinates when the need arises and shall not defer until Evaluation Reports are due.

Evaluation by the rater and endorser must be based upon actual records and reports, observation, and assessment of the rated officer in the performance of his duties, in his actions and reactions, and in the manner, he carries out his obligations. It should not be based on a few isolated or striking incidents. Ln the absence of facts on estimated performance or various duties on which to base a rating, no rating should be made. The current status of the efficiency of an organization will not be the sole basis for judgment by a military superior as to the effectiveness of the commander thereof. The degree to which the effectiveness of an officer is reflected in the efficiency of his organization will be measured in direct proportion of his opportunities for influencing the organization with consideration being given to the time element and with due allowance for factors beyond the control of the rated individual.

Through the report, the rated officer will be evaluated in comparison with others of similar grade.

The endorser s evaluations are of equal weight and importance with those of the rate. The endorser makes an independent evaluation of the rated officer, which should reflect his considered opinion of the rater. When the endorser receives a report containing entries in his judgment that are not warranted, whether favorable or adverse to the rated individual, the endorser should incorporate his views in his "comments" on the Evaluation Report.

Following are the parameters and their adjectival equivalents:

Rating	Adjectival Equivalent
10 (Outstanding)	The rated officer excels prominently and conspicuously in all activities of his unit. He is a stand out in suitability, service, and performance.
9 (Superior)	The rated officer maintains a very high standard of performance in all areas of his job. He contributes exceedingly well to other areas.
8 (Excellent)	The rating officer maintains a high standard of performance in all areas of his job. He contributes very well to other areas.
7 (Very Satisfactory)	The rated officer always meets all job requirements and excels in most areas of his job.
6 (Satisfactory)	The rated officer sufficiently meets all job requirements. He excels in certain areas of his job.
5 (Average)	The rated officer meets normal requirements and job standards. May need further training and self-improvement if he is to assume higher responsibility.
4 (Barely Satisfactory)	The rated officer is sometimes deficient in important job requirements and standards. Needs further training and self-improvement if he needs to remain in the present job.
3 (Bare Acceptable)	The rated officer is deficient in suitability and service reputation. Sometimes fails in important job

requirements. Badly needs further training and self-improvement to boast his little growth potentials.

2 (Unsatisfactory)	The rated officer is grossly deficient in performance or service reputation. Often rails in important job requirements. Has very little growth potentials. Should be considered for attrition.
1 (Unacceptable)	The rated officer is grossly deficient in performance and service reputation. Usually fails in all job requirements. Must be attrited.
0 (Unknown)	The rated/endorser does not know the performance, suitability, or service reputation of the rated officer.

Unfavorable Entries - Whenever an Evaluation Report contains entries below average 1, 2, 3 & 4 which may be considered in any sense unfavorable, the reason for the entry will be clearly stated, the rater shall refer the entire report direct to the rated officer for his remarks. The rated officer will immediately return it to the rating officer by endorsement with his remarks about the unfavorable entries only. The report will then be forwarded to the endorser by the rater with his remarks concerning the remarks of the rated officer. If the endorser has new unfavorable remarks on the rated officer, the entire report with its endorsements will be referred directly to the rated officer. The rated officer will forward the entire report with his comments and/or explanations to the endorser, through the rater. If the report is delayed when referred to the rated officer, a brief memorandum explaining the clarification will be attached. Likewise, a rating of 10 (Outstanding), justification(s) by the rater/endorser to be attached to the OER.

Release of Information - Evaluation Reports will be furnished only to personnel boards and career management authorities for use at Major Service headquarters level and above, for personnel actions. Any officer only on active duty or his authorized representative may examine his Evaluation Report file at any time by applying in person at The Adjutant General's Office, GHQ, AFP, or at the Major Service Adjutant General Office.

Formal Instruction - The PMA and all service schools in the ATP will include in the curricula of all officer courses being given therein, at least a two (2) hour formal instruction on the proper preparation and accomplishment of Evaluation Reports.

CIRCULAR NUMBER 16   13 September 1993

Enlisted Personnel Evaluation Marks

The Enlisted Personnel Evaluation Marks is designed to provide the AFP with a means of measuring the efficiency and effectiveness of an EP in the performance of his job.

Purpose:

To enhance professionalism among the EP. It will also provide an accurate measurement of the performance of EP under them. The Enlisted Personnel Evaluation Marks (EPEM) shall be used as one of the criteria for promotion, reenlistment, schooling (local and abroad), selection for key positions, and retention/separation from the service.

This circular applies to all enlisted personnel of the AFP.

Procedure:

a. All EP shall be rendered an EPEM at the end of June and December by two (2) raters and one (1) endorser.

b. Members of a squad or its equivalent in the Navy and the Air Force shall be rated by their Squad Leader and Platoon Sergeant with the Platoon Leader as endorser;

c. Squad Leader or their equivalent in the PN and the PAF shall be rated by their Platoon Sergeant and the Platoon Leader with the Company Ex-0 as the endorser;

d. Platoon Sergeant shall be rated by their respective First Sergeant and Platoon Leader with the Company Commander as the endorser,

e. Battalion/Group Sgt Major shall be rated by the Brigade Sgt Major and Battalion EX-O with the Battalion Commander as the endorser;

f. Battalion/Group Sgt Major shall be rated by the Brigade Sgt Major and Battalion EX-O with the Battalion Commander as the endorser;

g. Brigade Sgt Major shall be rated by the Division Sgt Major and the Deputy Brigade Commander with the Brigade Commander as the endorser;

h. Division/Regimental/another subordinate unit Sgt Major shall be rated by the Command Sgt Major and the Division/Regiment/other subordinate units Chief of Staff with the Division/Regiment/other subordinate Units Commander as the endorser,

i. Section NCO shall be rated by the Branch NCO and the Division Chief Clerk with the Branch Chief as endorser;

j. Branch NCO shall be rated by the Division Chief Clerk and the Branch Chief with the Deputy Chief of Office as the endorser;

k. Division Chief Clerks shall be rated by the Admin Officer and the Deputy Chief of office with the Chief of office as the endorser;

l. All other positions not covered above shall be rated by the next higher NCO in the chain of command and another officer and will be endorsed by his Commanding Officer.

m. In the event, that thru judgment of his immediate officer, the rater may not be able to judiciously rate the EP or there is doubt on the rating made by his immediate ranking NCO, then he will be rated by the next ranking superior who can judiciously rate the concerned EP or if warranted by his peers. If the latter is adopted there should be a minimum of three (3) raters. Moreover, this should be done confidentially.

Rating and Criteria

The raters and endorsers will rate the individual according to the following table:

RATING	EQUIVALENT POINTS	
Outstanding (Stands out among contemporaries)	4.6	5.0
Excellent (Rarely equaled by contemporaries)	4.1	4.5
Very Satisfactory (Equaled by a few of his/her Contemporaries)	3.6	4.0
Satisfactory (Equaled by majority of his/her Contemporaries)	3.1	3.5
Average (Just enough to meet Normal standards)	2.6	3.0
Fair (Needs Improvement)	2.1	2.5
Unsatisfactory (Incomplete)	2.0 and below	

CRITERIA	GRANTED POINTS
a. Proficiency in rate (Competence attention and Performance of duty)	----------------------
b. Conduct (Loyalty, enthusiasm, progressiveness, Open mindedness and disposition)	----------------------
c. Initiative (Vision, decisiveness, self-reliance, does not wait to be told)	----------------------
d. Morality (Integrity, sobriety, honor, trustworthiness	----------------------
e. Appearance (Military bearing, Neatness and self-confidence)	----------------------
f. Expression (Oral and written ability to communicate effectively)	----------------------
g. Personal Relations (Cooperation, tact, amount of respect received)	----------------------
h. Personal Traits (Temper, fairness, punctuality, sense of humor)	----------------------
i. Social Presence (Courtesy, good manner and proper decorum	----------------------

j. Physical Fitness (Endurance to military
    related training, fitness/capacity to perform
    both combat and office duties.   ----------------------

In cases where reassignment of personnel is made, rendition of special EPEM shall be accomplished and forwarded to the gaming unit to include his EPEM for the last three (3) years.

LEGEND/DEFINITION

A. RATING SCALE:

10   Outstanding - Rated officer prominently and conspicuously in all activities of his unit, stands out in suitability, service reputation, and performance.

9   Superior - Rated off maintains very high standards of performance in all areas of his job, contributes
exceedingly well m the other areas.

8   Excellent - Rated officer maintains a high standard of performance in all areas of his job Contributes very
well in other areas.

7   Very Satisfactory - Rated officer always meets and excels in most areas of his job.

6   Satisfactory - Rated officer sufficiently meets all job requirements and excel in certain areas of his job.

5   Average - Rated officer meets normal requirements and job standards. Needs further training and self
improvement to be able to assume higher responsibilities.

4   Barely Satisfactory - Rated officer is so efficient on important job requirements and standards. Needs further training and self-improvement to remain in the present job.

3   Barely Acceptable - Rated officer is deficient in performance and service reputation. Sometimes fails
important job requirements. Has very little growth potentials. Should be considered for attention.

2   Unsatisfactory - rated officer is grossly deficient in performance and service reputation. Often fails
important job requirements. Has very' little growth potentials. Should be considered for attention.

1   Unacceptable - The rated officer is grossly deficient in performance and service reputation. Usually fails in all job requirements.' Must be tinted.

0   Unknown - Rater/Endorser does not know the performance suitability or service reputation of the rated officer.

B. DEFINITION OF TRAITS

Suitability - refers to the qualifications of the rated officer for the job in terms of his academic preparation, experience, mental and physical health.

1. Leadership - inspire confidence and exerts a strong influence.
2. Management - organization and utilization of men, money & materials.
3. Mental - reasoning alertness, judgment, common sense, adaptability.
4. Physical - health, strength, energy, build, voice, agility, endurance.
5. Power of spoken expression - speaks or instruct effectively.
6. Power of written expression - clear, concise, and correct
7. Profession Knowledge & background — well - rounded and informed
8. Psychological Stamina - moral and physical courage, presence of mind in an emergency, under great strain, or prolonged pressure.

Service Reputation - refers to the demeanor and character traits of the rated officer about his job as he is known in the unit, intermediate headquarters, and/or the whole command.

1. Attention to Duty and Acceptance of Responsibility.
2. Attitude - loyalty, enthusiasm, progressiveness, open-mindedness, disposition.
3. Initiative — vision, decisiveness, self-reliance, does not wait to be told.
4. Morality - integrity', sobriety', trustworthiness, code of conduct.
5. Personal appearance and military presence.
6. Personal relations - cooperation, tact, amount of respect received.
7. Personal traits - temper, fairness, punctuality, sense of humor.
8. Social Presence - courtesy, good manners & decorum proper to the occasion.

GO FORM 67-m Incl D to Cir Nr 22 did 14 Oct 87

Promotion

Promotion is the advancement of an employee to a better job involving greater responsibility, greater prestige, greater skills, higher pay, and better hours, or better working conditions.

It involves the reassignment of an employee to a higher-level job. When promoted, employees generally face increasing demands in terms of skills, abilities, and responsibilities. In turn, employees generally receive increased pay and (sometimes) benefits as well as greater authority and status.

A position becomes vacant when a person occupying that position dies, resigns, retires, or is terminated. Whenever a position becomes vacant, the employees within the organization (intra-organization) who occupy the next- in-rank-position shall be considered for promotion. However, the appointing authority may promote an employee who is occupying a next-in-rank-position who possesses a superior qualification and competence compared to a next-in-rank employee who merely meets the minimum requirements for the position or the appointing authority may appoint somebody from other organizations (inter-organization) if there is no qualified employee in the organization where the vacancy exists.

An open promotion system enables greater use of employee skills and abilities as compared to a closed system. Criteria for making promotion decisions should be applied in a manager consistent with the nature of the work and organizational goals. Seniority and performance are prime factors in making promotions among employees.

Assessment centers are valuable tools for identifying potential managers among non-managerial personnel. Political considerations, though impossible to eliminate, should be minimized.

Decision-makers must write sound personnel policies for making internal-staffing decisions. An important issue to clarify is whether to promote from within or hire from outside. Normally, the advantages of promoting from within far outweigh the other.

Purposes of Transfer and Promotion Programs

To increase the effectiveness of the organization in attaining its service and profit objectives.

Personal nature or they are used to keep the promotion ladder open and to keep individuals' interest in the work. Employee's talents and training may be put to more effective use.

Job changes provide an opportunity for present employees to move into jobs that provide an opportunity for present employees to move into jobs that provide greater compensation, personal satisfaction, and prestige. Being transferred to a new job may open up new avenues of advancement or add the spice of variety to daily routines. Of course, not all employees want to be transferred or promoted. Many like the assurance of settled security; yet, most like to feel that opportunities for transfer or promotion are available.

Many middle managers reach a plateau simply because there is no room for all of them at the top. Many employees improve their qualifications by taking evening courses, attending seminars, or doing self-study in the hope that they can be considered for promotion or transfer to a job which will give them greater satisfaction or better employment status.

They are used to give people broader job experiences as part of their development and to fill vacancies as they occur. Employees are transferred from one job to another on a rotation basis to allow them to learn other jobs and thus broaden their knowledge about the company's operations.

Inadequately performing employees may be transferred to other jobs simply because a higher-level manager is reluctant to demote or separate them.

Bases for promotion

Job analysis provides information on the skill, experience, training, responsibility, and environmental factors involved in each job. Comparing such information for various jobs shows which jobs have similar requirements. Then, on each specification, the other jobs from and to which changes can logically be made are listed.

If a particular person filling a job has the qualifications to enter another line of progression, this should be permitted. This is a matter of personal qualifications and does not destroy the validity of natural job relationships.

When job relationships have been fully explored, it is wise to construct a promotion chart. To determine job requirements, use the job description and job specification.

Performance and ability or potential, are the two principal criteria for determining promotions. Performance refers to the individual's productivity in his present position. Potential or ability refers to how well the individual will perform when placed in a new position of authority and responsibility.

Promotion within the ranks should be done whenever possible. In case there are no candidates for a vacancy in the same unit, a search for any candidate within the company should be made.

Closed Promotion System

The more common approach is the closed promotion system, which places the responsibility for identifying promotable employees with the supervisor of the job to be filled. In addition to reviewing the past performance and assessing the potential of subordinates, a supervisor may require in other departments about employees who may be qualified for the job. A drawback to the closed promotion system is that many employees who may be qualified and interested in the promotion are often overlooked.

Open Promotion System

This is an approach that overcomes the problem of the closed promotion system. This system is popularly known as the job posting. With job posting, job vacancies are publicized on bulletin boards and internal communication systems so that all interested employees may apply. Job posting enhances participation and equal opportunity, but it also increases administrative expenses and takes time.

Types of Promotion (Andres, 1991)

Vertical Promotion. This is a promotion from one rank to the next in the same department. If a company is organized into a few major departments, this plan of promotion has fewer disadvantages than if it is subdivided into numerous specialized units. In the latter case, it limits both the experience and the opportunity of an employee because he has only a limited contract with the business as a whole.

Horizontal Promotion. Under this plan, an employee may be transferred from a position in one department to a position of higher rank or of the same rank in another department. Horizontal promotion is most easily followed in a company that has several units performing similar activities.

Promotion Criteria

For many employees, promotion is a highly sought prize. Climbing the organizational ladder has long been a part of the American dream. Status, satisfaction, and financial rewards accrue to those who can rise in an organization. But frustration, stress, and even severe depression may occur when personal goals of upward mobility are unheeded by an organization-particularly when an employee feels passed over for a deserved promotion. Because organizational effectiveness and job satisfaction are influence by the way promotions are made, organizations need to gather reliable data for making decisions about promotions. There are several criteria that organizations officially examine in deciding which candidate to promote.

Two General Types of Seniority (Sison, 1991)

Straight Seniority - means that length of service alone determines employment preference. It is a policy whereby a man with the longest service is given priority in job opportunities, such as promotions and transfers. Unions often advocated such a policy because it is much easier to determine seniority than merit or ability. The unions' interpretation of seniority is that the employee with the longest service should get the promotion or be retained in the payroll during periods of forced cutdowns in preference to the other men who may be equally or even better qualified to perform the work but who have had fewer years of continuous service in the firm.

Qualified Seniority - means that the length of service is just one of several specified factors used to determine preference in employment opportunities. Employees who are efficient, capable, and who have shown good performance in their jobs drawn upon the straight seniority rule. Other factors considered are educational attainment, fitness for the job as shown in the tests, training, and experience in the type of job to be filled, and efficiency in the present job. Qualified seniority gives merit or efficiency greater weight than plain seniority.

Policy on Seniority

The adoption of a sound company policy on the matter of seniority is important to good employee relations. If policies are clear-cut and carefully written, many employee gripes will be presented. A definite policy, for instance, should specify whether merit and seniority will be given equal weight or whether or not one will take precedence over the other. It should also indicate under what conditions seniority rights are acquired, retained, and terminated, and it should as well define their limits.

The policy should likewise state if management will be given sufficient latitude to promote, retain, and rehire employees because of their skill, ability, and experience. The policy should provide answers to questions regarding how seniority will be affected by absences, sickness, layoffs, accidents, broken service, or what employment rights and privileges will go with promotion, demotion, and transfer.

Assessment Center

To improve the chances of making successful promotional decisions - particularly from non-management to management - many organizations are using assessment centers. Job candidates are brought to assessment centers for evaluation of their promotability, as measured by a series of exercises. These exercises focus on the kind of skills and abilities required to effectively perform the higher-level jobs that the candidates seek.

The primary purpose of the assessment center is to improve an organization's selection of managers, particularly at the first level of management A secondary purpose is to increase the pool of employees from which managers are selected.

Unofficial Promotion Criteria

A common retort to a presentation of official criteria used in promotion decisions is this "What you say about making promotional decisions is all well and good, but it's all theory. Where I work, promotions depend on who you know, not what you do." The statement contains a good deal of truth. All too often, a gulf exists between theory and practice when promotions are considered. Rational criteria such as seniority, performance, and assessment center ratings may be cast aside for political reasons. Unofficial criteria may influence or even dominate a promotion decision.

Personal Characteristics

Together, Title VII of the Civil Rights Act and the Age Discrimination Act Prohibit discrimination in all terms and conditions of employment based on age, race, color, religion, sex, or national origin. All internal-staffing decisions fall under the domain of these acts, just as external recruiting, selection, and placement practices do. Although almost all organizations profess to abide by EEO guidelines and include Equal Opportunity Employer" at the bottom of their help-wanted advertisements, not all organizations practice what they preach. Certain personal characteristics of the candidate may either help or hinder progression into the upper levels of the organization. Being of the "wrong" sex, race, or religion may create a real though unspoken obstacle to advancement. Such practices are not only immoral and unethical but also clearly illegal. Prejudice causes a sizable pool of valuable human talent to be overlooked and wasted.

Nepotism

Being of a certain bloodline sometimes helps one's progression into a higher-level job. Nepotism, from the Italian nepotism ("favoriting of nephews"), is the showing of favoritism or patronage to relatives. Nepotism is often criticized because family members get desirable jobs and promotions primarily under their lineage. Nepotism is still practiced by many well-known firms.

Social Factors

Membership in a certain club or political party, graduation from the right university, and participation in the right sport (traditionally golf, perhaps now jogging, tennis, or racquetball) are important in getting promoted in some organizations, particularly at the upper-management and staff levels.

Friendship

In organizations of all forms and sizes, strong informal bonds are created between employees who share common interests, ideals, values, beliefs., and attitudes. In turn, such informal bonds between decision-makers and candidates for promotion may play a significant role in deciding who gets promoted and who doesn't. Particularly at the top organizational levels, executives prefer to work with people whose thoughts and perceptions mirror their own. In a sense, this personal chemistry may be just as important as the ability in getting ahead.

Promotion Policies

Promotion is done to increase the overall efficiency of the organization and to aid in the personal development and interest of the employees.

A good policy should contain:

A statement of management's intention that higher paid and better jobs will be filled by promotion from within whenever possible, rather than by hiring from outside the organization.

Encouragement for superiors to permit capable employees to leave the unit if better opportunities are available elsewhere. If a good employee is held back, he is not likely to remain satisfied. An open job-bidding system encourages internal mobility.

Progression ladders of promotion are established within the organization. Job analysis can be used to develop a chart showing basic job requirements (incompetence, experience, formal education, etc.) and how each job leads to another. Employees need to know what is expected in higher-rated jobs to prepare themselves for advancement.

Line responsibility for making promotions should be established with the advice and assistance of the Human Resource Department in a staff capacity. The supervisor should propose promotions, which should then be subject to approval by his immediate superior. This serves as a check on the fairness of promotion and ensures that the policy will be consistently administered.

Provisions for employee or union challenge of a particular promotion should be included in the promotion policy and the union agreement. Ordinarily, the management or a Human Resource Manager who always adhered to a sound promotion policy has little to fear.

Two procedures that are important for the success of a promotion policy are:

Posting a notice of opening for promotions, so that interested employees may apply within a specified period, usually several days or a week. If possible, the news should be posted and the candidates selected before the job becomes vacant. If the job is temporarily filled by an employee who is subsequently advanced to the job permanently, the other applicants are likely to feel that the posting procedure is a farce.

Provision for training as a means of preparation for promotion. Special on-the-job training school's night classes or vocational courses, as well as special retraining programs, should be available. The changing job requirements in an age of science and technology require extensive retraining of employees if they are to qualify for better jobs.

To ensure the qualification and competence of the employee, the following requirements will be considered to determine the qualified candidates:

1. Performance - this shall be based on the last performance rating of the employee and should have at least a very satisfactory rating. This performance is essential in predicting his/her probable success in the position he/she is aspiring to.

2. Education and Training —Education and training should be relevant to the position. These include the educational background and successful completion of training courses, scholarships, training grants, and others.

3. Experience and Outstanding Accomplishment - these shall include occupational history, work experience, and accomplishments worthy of special commendations.

4. Physical Characteristics and Personal Traits - these refer to physical fitness, attitudes, and personality traits.

5. Potential - this takes into account the employee's capability not only to perform the duties and assume the responsibilities of the position to be filled but also those of higher and more responsible positions.

The objectivity in promotion is the task of the Promotion or Selection Board (PSB), established in every department or agency to adopt formal screening procedures and formulate criteria for the evaluation of candidates for promotion. Members of the PSB shall evaluate the qualifications of an employee following the agency Merit Promotion Plan. In filling supervisory positions, the PSB shall develop criteria for managerial and leadership to form part of the selection instrument. No other Civil Service eligibility shall be required for promotion to a higher position at the same level and within the same functionally related grouping of position (Omnibus Rules). Employees with a pending administrative case shall be disqualified for promotion during the pendency thereof and if found guilty, shall be disqualified for promotion for the period based on the penalty.

The promotions of officers are based on the Standard Operating Procedure (SOP) Number 10 known as the Officers Promotion system. The SOP embodies the rules policies, procedures, and guidelines governing the promotions of all officers in the active service.

The AFP Officers Promotions System espouses the concept that officers shall be selected for promotion based on their relative seniority, professional attributes, demonstrated performance and behavior, and their indicated potentials to discharge the duties and responsibilities of the next higher grade. This is to ensure that the military executives possess the necessary skills, expertise, and leadership qualities to perform their functions in the various units.

To be qualified for promotion, the officer must possess all the necessary completion of required Time-in-Grade (TIG), military career courses inclusion in the Zone of Consideration (next in line in promotion list) prescribed for each grade, and Position Eligibility.

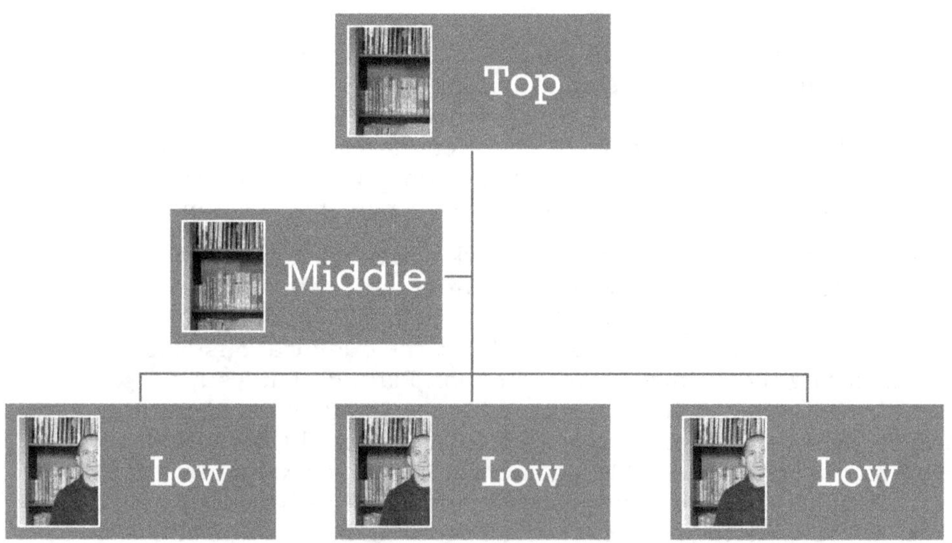

Chapter IV

COMPENSATION
Compensation is a part of the transaction between an employee and an employer that results in an employment contract. Compensation refers to all forms of payment going to employees of all levels and arising from employment.

Good managers can turn straw to gold. Poor managers can do the reverse. This realization has not been lost on those who design a compensation system for the organization. Managers tend to be more highly pain than operatives. As a manager's authority and responsibility expand, so typically does his or her pay. Moreover, many organizations willingly offer extremely lucrative compensation packages to get and keep good managers (Robbins, 1988).

Compensation is the financial remuneration given by the organization to its employees in exchange for their work. There are three basic forms of compensation. Wage is the hourly compensation pain to operating employees. Salary refers to compensation paid for total contributions, as opposed to being based on hour work. For example, managers earn an annual salary, usually paid monthly. They receive the salary regardless of the number of hours they work. Some firms have started paying all their employees a salary instead of hourly wages. Finally, incentives represent special compensation opportunities that are usually tied to performance. Sales commissions and bonuses are among the most common incentives (Griffin, 1996).

The goals of compensation policies include rewarding employees' performance, being competitive in the labor market, attracting new employees, maintaining equity among employees, and increasing job satisfaction and possibly the motivational level of employees. A goal in non-union organizations is also to have a compensation package attracting enough to keep out a union (Drummond, 1990).

Wages and Salaries
Many factors affect how wages and salaries are set. These factors include what is currently being paid in the area, the labor market, the minimum wage and other government regulations, the worth of the job, the cost of living, the employer's ability to pay, and the presence of a collective bargaining agreement, Pay rates are often adjusted upward to help employees cope with inflation. Cost-of-living adjustment (COLA) is seen in union contracts and also in the policies of many nonunion organizations. Usually, COLA is based on the consumer price index (CPI), a government measure of the average change in prices over a certain period for goods and services that people buy day-to-day living (Drummond, 1990).

Objectives of Wages and Incentives
1. To grade jobs in relationships with each other, to some established base, or similar jobs on other plants with frequent examination results.
2. To formulate wage scales for each job classification.

3. To consider payment of bonuses to supervisory personnel.
4. To consider effective means of stimulating and rewarding executives
5. To provide for stability of employment in so far as possible, through careful scheduling of operations and financial planning.

Kinds of Employee Compensation

Salary - refers to the compensation covering weekly, monthly, or yearly periods for services rendered. The term applies to the pay of higher levels of personnel such as white-collar employees or persons in positions of responsibility and authority in the firm.

Wages - refers to compensation for manual labor-skilled or unskilled - for work done by so-called "blue-collar" workers. Wages are measured by the hour, day, or week, unlike salaries which are paid at stated intervals, such as every week or every fifteen days. Wages also refer to payment for a specified volume of production, i.e. on piece rate.

Incentive pay - is a kind of compensation designed to encourage the employee to render extra effort over normal production.

Employee benefits or fringe benefits are supplemental compensation that employees receive, aside from their direct wages or incentive pay. These benefits represent labor costs over and above straight time earning. They are granted to an employee to provide them with facilities and assistance and are either voluntarily granted by the company by the company or a part of the collective bargaining agreement or required by law. They are given to employees regardless of the difference in individual performance.

Criteria for Compensation Effectiveness

For compensation to be effective, it should be:

Adequate - Minimum governmental, union and managerial levels should be met.

Equitable - Each person should be paid fairly, in line with his or her effort, abilities, and training.

Balanced - Pay, benefits, and other rewards should provide a reasonable total package.

Cost-Effective - Pay is not excessive, considering what the organization can afford to pay.

Secure - pay should be enough to help an employee feel secure and aid him or her in satisfying basic needs.

Incentive providing - Pay should motivate effective and productive work.

Compensation and Benefits

Laws also regulate compensation and benefits. The Fair Labor Standard Act, passed in 1938 and amended frequently since then, sets a minimum wage and requires the payment of overtime rates for work over forty hours per week. Salaried professional, executive, and administrative employees are exempt from minimum hourly wage and overtime provisions. The Equal Pay Act of 1963 requires that men and women perform the same amount for doing the same jobs. Attempts to circumvent the law by having different job titles and pay rates for men and women who perform the same work are also illegal. Basing an employee's pay on seniority or performance, however, is legal even if it means that a man and woman are paid different amounts for doing the same job.

The provision of benefits is also regulated in some ways by state and federal laws. Certain benefits are mandatory – for example, worker's compensation insurance for employees who are required on the job. Employers who provide a pension plan for their employees are regulated by the Employee Retirement Income Security Act of 1974 (ERISA). The purpose of this act is to help ensure the financial security of pension funds by regulating how they can be invested. The Family and Medical Leave Act of 1993 requires employers to provide up to twelve weeks of unpaid leave for family and medical emergencies (Griffin, 1996).

The Legal Environment of HRM (Griffin, 1996)
Area of Regulation

Equal Employment Opportunity
Title VII of the Civil Rights Act of 1994 (as amended by the Equal Employment Opportunity Act of 1972): Forbids discrimination in all areas of the employment relationship

Age Discrimination in Employment Act: Outlaws discrimination against people older than 40 years

Various executive orders, especially Executive Order 11246 in 1965: Requires employers with government contracts to engage in affirmative action

Pregnancy Discrimination Act: Specifically, outlaws' discrimination based on pregnancy

Vietnam Era Veterans Readjustment Assistance Act: Extends affirmative action mandate to military veterans who served during the Vietnam war

Americans With Disability Act: Specifically, outlaws' discrimination against disabled persons

Civil Rights Act of 1991: Makes it easier for employees to sue an organization for discrimination, but limits punitive awards if the win

Compensation and Benefits
Fair Labor Standards Act: Establishes minimum wage and mandated overtime pay for work over 40 hours per week

Equal Pay Act: Requires that men and women be paid the same amount for doing the same job

Employee Retirement Income Security Act: Requires how organizations manage their pension funds

Family and Medical Leave Act of 1993: Requires employers to provide up to 12 weeks of unpaid leave for family and medical emergencies

Labor Relations
National Labor Relations Act: Establishes procedures by which employees can establish labor unions and requires organizations to bargain collectively with legally formed unions; also known as the Wagner Act

Labor-Management Relations Act: Limits union power and specifies management rights during a union-organizing campaign; also known as the Taft-Hartley Act

Health and Safety
Occupational Safety and Health Act: Mandates the provision of safe working conditions

The level of unemployment in the labor force also affects wage levels. Pay declines when labor is plentiful and increases when labor is scarce.

In her book, Human Resources Management for the Hospitality Industry, Karen Drummond discussed job evaluation, government regulation of compensation, and the legally required benefits:

Job Evaluation
Job evaluation is the systematic process of determining the relative worth of jobs in an organization, then determining which jobs should pay more than others. Job evaluation also helps establish which jobs have the same worth to the organization. Because job evaluation is used to set up a salary structure, it is crucial to job satisfaction and productivity.

Government Regulation of Compensation
The major federal law regarding wages is the Fair Labor Standards Act (FLSA), commonly called the Wage and Hour Act or the federal minimum wage law. The major parts of the act are concerned with the minimum wage, child labor protections, and equal rights as stated in the Equal Pay Act of 1963 and the Age Discrimination in Employment Act of 1967.

Legally Required Benefits
Legally required benefits include Social Security, worker's compensation, and unemployment compensation. Congress passed the first phase of the Social Security program in 1935. The program is divided into four major parts:

old-age benefits, disability benefits, survivors' benefits, and Medicaid. The employee pays a fixed percentage of his or her income (in 1990, 7.65 percent of the first $57,000 earned) to the federal government, and the employer pays a similar amount.

Old-age benefits start at age sixty-five, but this is being raised gradually to sixty-seven years of age. To receive old-age benefits, an individual must have worked for at least ten years. Persons under seventy who are collecting Social Security payments and are also gainfully employed can earn only so much income before having to pay back some of it to Social Security.

Employees who had been disabled for at least six months will be disabled for at least twelve more months and have worked and paid into Social Security for at least five years are also eligible to receive Social Security payments. It is computed similarly to retirement benefits.

Dependents of retired disabled, or deceased workers are entitled to receive Social Security payments if under eighteen years of age and not married. Other survivors may qualify for payment as well. Medicare is an amendment to the Social Security Act and is usually treated as a separate program from Social Security. Medicare's primary purpose is to help people sixty-five and older pay for health care costs.

Workers' compensation law intends to provide the cost of medical expenses and income to individuals who become hurt on the job. The payment of workers' compensation insurance is compulsory in most states. Depending on state laws. Employers may insure with private companies, join a state insurance system, or become self-insured. The premiums, which the employer usually pays, depend to a large extent on the company's safety record.

Unemployment Compensation refers to benefits paid to employees who are laid off from a job for up to twenty-six weeks. These employees must register to receive the compensation and be willing to accept any suitable employment offered. The employee's most recent wage and period of employment determines the amount of the benefits. Both the federal and the state governments collect an amount based on percentages of each employee's wages, up to an established maximum; most of the federal money is returned to the states to operate the program.

Chapter V

INTEGRATION
Meriam-Webster dictionary defines integration as the act or process or an instance of integrating: such as a: incorporation as equals into society or an organization of individuals of different groups (such as races) b: coordination of mental processes into a normal effective personality or with the environment.

Discipline
Management in an adversarial environment stresses organizational punishment as the principal method of achieving employee discipline. Like the benevolent parent who spanks an errant child, the parental manager punishes the deficient employee. Employers used the term progressive discipline, to describe the process of administering more severe punishment for more serious deficiencies and for less serious ones that are repeated. The work progressive, however, does not mean advanced or enlightened; it simply means the use of harsher punishment.

Cooperative management uses progressive discipline, but only as a last resort. Instead, management relies upon methods, such as positive reinforcement and job structuring, to develop employee self-discipline. Also, instead of progressive discipline, some companies are using a new method, called positive discipline, in helping shape employee behavior.

Discipline is employee learning that promotes self-control, dedication, and orderly conduct. Discipline is generally used in a restricted sense to mean punishment Consequently, the written procedures used to punish employees for job deficiencies are called disciplinary procedures.

Punishment is defined as the process of either administering an unpleasant stimulus, such as a warning letter or a suspension, or withholding a reward, such as not granting a scheduled pay increase because of an employee's job deficiencies. Punishment is only one form of discipline; other forms are positive reinforcement, such as commendations and praise, and human resources development.

Sources of Employee Discipline
Three Sources of Discipline

Self	Group	Employer
Maturation	Norms	Human Resources Development
Goals	Status	Performance Appraisal
Needs	Roles	Rewards
		Punishment

The best types of discipline are that which is exercised through self-control Self- discipline is generally achieved through maturation. As people mature, they learn to accept responsibility for their actions. This learning process includes following the examples set by role models, such as parents and teachers. Peoples' goals and needs, such as a need for recognition, also influence their self-discipline. Employers can help employees meet these needs through various methods, including relatively simple ones such as having them write their names on an article they produce to give them credit for their work.

Employee workgroups influence member's behavior through the establishment of norms, assignment of roles, and conferring status. Norms are standards of employee behavior to which members are expected to adhere. These standards may include how much an employee is expected to produce, how the employee is expected to behave on the job, and whether an employee is supposed to cooperate with management. The more cohesive the workgroup, that is the degree to which employees associate with the group and seek acceptance from it, the more the group can influence an employee's work role perceptions. Sometimes, group influence can cause employees to behave in ways contrary to the best interests of a firm. Unions can have an especially powerful influence on employee behavior, both good and bad.

Methods for Reducing the Number of Personnel

Layoffs - the most direct method of reducing the number of personnel. Great care should be taken in making layoff decisions to avoid age discrimination violations. Layoffs typically produce a great deal of anxiety, thus the employees to be laid off should be named as soon as possible and given advance notice for them to plan.

Attrition - sometimes called restrictive hiring refers to reducing the workforce by failing to replace individuals who leave. If enough planning has been done, an organization may avoid layoffs simply through attrition; only those replacements that are essential to the organization are made.

Reduced Hours - If the labor surplus appears to be a short-term problem, many organizations prefer to reduce the number of hours each employee works and keep all of the employees.

Early Retirement - an organization that has several employees who are nearing retirement age may be able to reduce its workforce by encouraging older employees to take early retirement. To encourage early retirement, however, an organization must frequently offer financial incentives that may offset the savings that might have been accrued by reducing the workforce.

Human Resource Development

As stated at the beginning of this discussion on discipline, HRD is essential to employee discipline because it is the HRM activity completely committed, to employee learning. HRD helps prevent employee deficiencies since it teaches employees both how to perform their job tasks and the job conduct and attendance standards that they are expected to meet.

Performance Appraisal. An essential aspect of performance appraisal is establishing expected standards of behavior for each performance variable. Performance expectations are communicated to employees and their performance is appraised through the appraisal system. The employee's performance is either rewarded or punished as the circumstances warrant.

Rewards. Employees receive intrinsic and extrinsic rewards from their job performance. Extrinsic rewards discipline employee performance through positive reinforcement. Merit pay systems reward employees for overall job performance in attendance, conduct, productivity, safety, and work quality. Employees who observe management equitably basing such rewards upon performance are motivated to perform better. General pay increases and those based upon the length of service do not instill self-discipline in job performance because there is no link between those rewards and performance outcomes.

Punishment. It is another alternative employer use in disciplining employees. It should be remembered in reviewing that the word discipline is the one employer invariably use to mean punishment.

The second part of punishment procedures is educating employees to follow the procedures. Usually, this step is accomplished by disseminating the procedures in the employee handbook and regularly publishing various provisions in the employee newsletter and other communication media. The rules and provisions disseminated most frequently are related to those deficiencies occurring often, such as absenteeism.

Meeting Punishment

The effective use of punishment requires supervisors to follow several steps discussed below.

A. Understand the Rules and Performance Criteria

Consistent application of rules and other performance criteria among supervisors requires them to have a uniform understanding of them. To obtain this understanding, supervisors typically receive extensive Human Resource Development (HRD) aimed at learning the rules and other criteria and how to interpret them. For example, the author was conducting a performance appraisal session with a group of higher-level managers in one organization. The session included setting criteria for performance variables. There was a considerable difference of opinion among the managers concerning several criteria such as punctuality. One manager felt even one tardiness was inexcusable Another manager felt one tardiness each week, as long as the employee was not later than 10 minutes, was permissible. This example shows the difficulty in getting managers to understand and uniformly agree on specific criteria HRD can help control that problem.

HRD also usually includes simulations, such as role-playing sessions to give supervisors the interpersonal abilities in areas like oral communication, stress tolerance, and sensitivity, to deal successfully with deficient employees.

B. Set Criteria

The process of meeting punishment is in part related to employee performance appraisal. For example, employees need to be informed of performance standards so they can perform according to those expectations Naturally, employees do not need to be told not to steal but there are many performance criteria, such as expected levels of production and work quality, that can be quantified and explained to employees.

C. Uniformity Enforce Rules

Uniformly enforcing rules and other performance standards help prevent problems like grievances and discrimination complaints. When an apparent deficiency is underlined because the actual situation may not be fully understood until the facts are known, including the employee s explanation. Prompt action shows employees that standards are important and they are being given attention. The important point is not to overlook an incident and expect it to go away, but the greater likelihood is it will recur.

D. Get the Facts

Two important parts of meting punishment are determining and analyzing the facts and choosing the appropriate level of punishment based upon those facts. An employee who is punished may disagree with the type of punishment administered, but the facts used to make that decision should not be disputed.

The best type of facts is documentable ones, such as timecard entries that show tardiness or written evidence of errors. Supervisors also should prepare written descriptions of what occurred, if they were witnesses to an event.

An indispensable part of fact-gathering is obtaining the employee's opinion of what happened. Generally, disciplinary action should not be taken without allowing the employee to offer this explanation. The explanation, if any is given, should be in writing, should specifically address the alleged deficiency, and should be signed by the employee.

E. Take Prompt and Consistent Action

Punishment, like other methods of behavior modification, is most effective when it is promptly administered. Prolonged waiting causes employee apprehension and other problems because people forget important facts. Delay also is associated with indecisiveness which causes employees to question whether management is serious about requiring employees to meet performance standards.

Employers can be reasonable "tough" with employees, provided they are consistent in meeting punishment. Inconsistency causes feelings of unfairness which can result in charges of discrimination.

F. Help Employees

In all types of punishment except discharge, the supervisor's intent should be to help the employee improve. Unfortunately, in every organization, there is a small percentage of employees, probably less than 1 percent, who just seem unable or unwilling to improve. These individuals frustrate even the most patient and tolerant supervisor. These employees generally fit one or more of these categories, they have profound personal problems, such being a late-stage alcoholic; they are improperly placed in which case the job is either too demanding and they are unable to adequately perform the tasks or they are over-qualified and they are bored to the point of exasperation; or, they have a physical or mental handicap or conditions, such as an uncorrected vision problem that prevents them from performing adequately. Every effort should be made to diagnose these problems and help the employee but sometimes? even, the best help is to no avail leaving an employee with no alternative but to discharge the employee.

Types of Punishment

1. Informal punishment is for very minor deficiencies or infractions, is administered orally, and may or may not result in the supervisor making a written record. Two common forms of informal punishment are counseling an oral reprimand.

2. Counseling is the process of discussing a deficiency with an employee and attempting to advise the individual on how to improve. This punishment is for the most minor deficiencies which are usually unintentional and are not expected to recur.

3. Oral Reprimand is a more severe form of informal punishment in which the supervisor emphatically directs the employee's attention to orally warned "you after each of those absences that you are required to read the schedule and report as scheduled. I also explained to you that your unscheduled absences require me to call in other employees on overtime and prevent your shift from meeting production schedules."

Forms of Punishment

A. Suspension

The suspension is placing an employee in a non-pay status due to more serious and/or repeated deficiencies. A layoff is also placing an employee in a non-pay status, but it is used in situations where there is not enough work available rather than for performance deficiencies. Some organizations use the term disciplinary layoff for layoffs used for punishment purposes. Suspensions are short-term discharge since the period in which an employee is suspended is unpaid and is not counted for such purposes as retirement or vacation credit.

B. Demotion

A demotion is a personal action in which an employee is placed in a job at a salary range lower than the one he/she currently is in. Demotions can either be voluntary or involuntary. Among the voluntary reasons an employee may request a demotion include wanting to be relieved of the stress or the travel requirements of the job. Sometimes supervisors request demotions are caused by either a reduction-in-force or the need for punishment. Organizations reduce employment levels for such reasons as a sales slump or discontinuance of a product line. Sometimes in these cases, an employee will be demoted to another job to avert being placed on layoff.

C. Withholding Pay Increase

Withholding a pay increase is usually the result of an unsatisfactory performance rating- For example, in merit pay systems, such as those used for more jobs in the federal service, there is a progression of steps within each pay grade. Advancement to the next higher pay step is conditional upon an employee's "satisfactory performance during the requisite waiting period between stop increase.

Some HRM professionals feel withholding a pay increase is too severe because I adversely affect an employee's pay in the long term since it is not only delaying an immediate increase but also extends the waiting period for subsequent pay increases. For example, most procedures provide for a minimum withholding period, such as three months, after a decision is made not to grant an increase. During this period, the employee attempts to bring his/her performance up to expectations to the pay increase that can be granted. As noted above, this three-month postponement extends the waiting period for the pay increase and similarly delays all future increases. The cumulative effect of these delays upon an employee's income over his/her entire career can be significant.

D. Discharge

A discharge is terminating an employee's employment due to deficiencies. Discharges are reserved for only the most serious deficiencies and in cases where employees do not improve after repeated efforts are made to correct their behavior through less serious forms of punishment, such as reprimands, suspensions, and demotions.

Progressive Versus Positive Discipline

Despite the popularity of progressive discipline, there are some serious problems with it. First, it emphasizes procedures instead of people training supervisors in the lockstep manner of publishing employees rather than the human considerations of employee disciples. Consequently, punishment often only addresses the observable result, that is the deficiency and ignores the real problem, such as substance abuse, that may be contributing to the problem. Another problem with progressive discipline is that it treats employees like children. Third, in progressive discipline the employee is a passive party in the decision-making process, the supervisor observes the deficiency, considers any mitigation, makes a decision, informs the employee, and implements the decision. Finally, progressive discipline is best characterized by confrontation and conflict. The supervisor confronts the employee with the deficiency and then, usually, a tug-of-war begins from the conflict caused by the employee's resistance to the punishment received from the supervisor. These conflicts can generate considerable hostility and ill-feelings which is one reason why supervisors dislike progressive disciplinary procedures and thus sometimes avoid using them to the detriment of the organization.

A. Positive Discipline Defined

Positive discipline is the process of treating deficient employees as adults in improving their performance, and in some cases, providing decision-making for them to determine whether they will make a commitment to meet their job responsibilities within the company or should seek employment elsewhere.

B. Distinctions are Progressive and Positive Discipline

There are major distinctions between progressive discipline and positive discipline. First, as noted in Table 4, progressive discipline is. punishment but positive discipline is not.

Distinctions in Progressive and Positive Discipline

Type Area	Progressive Discipline	Positive Discipline
Type Discipline	Punishment	Self-discipline
Emphasis	Procedures	People
Ego States	Parent/child	Adult/adult
Decision-maker	Supervisor	Employee
Setting	Confront/conflict	Control/cooperate

In positive discipline, employees are sent "reminders" and not warnings or reprimands. Warnings and reprimands fit the definition of punishment because they are unpleasant stimuli but reminders are not. Also, employees are suspended without pay in progressive discipline but in positive discipline, employees are given a day's leave with pay; the purpose of the day is for the employee to conduct a self-assessment, evaluate his/her job responsibilities, and make a decision whether to meet those responsibilities or seek employment elsewhere. Also, in all cases except discharges, the deficient employee commits to the action he or she intends to take to correct the deficiency.

Application of Discipline in the AFP

Military Law

The Philippine Military Law provides the basic law for the discipline of the Armed Forces and the Manual for Court-Martial, AFP, prescribes the basic regulations governing its administration. The agencies through which military jurisdiction is exercised include:

Courts-Martial - General, special and summary for the trial of offenders against military law, and, in the case of general Courts-Martial, of persons who by the law of war are subject to trial by military tribunals;

Commanding Officers exercising disciplinary powers under A.W. 105;

Courts of inquiry for the examination of transactions of or accusations or imputation against officers or soldiers, and for such purposes or may be indicated by law and regulations.

Military Tribunals for the trial of offenses within their respective jurisdiction. Unless otherwise provided they shall be guided by the applicable rule of procedures and evidence prescribed for courts-martial.

Courts-Martial have exclusive jurisdictions of purely military offenses. The jurisdiction of courts-martial is entirely penal on disciplinary. They have no powers to adjudge the payments of damages or to collect private debts.

Courts-Martial are lawful tribunals, with authority to finally determine any case ever which they have jurisdictions, and their proceedings, when confirmed as provided, are not open to review by the civil tribunals, the military court has jurisdiction on the person and subject matter, and whether, through having such jurisdictions it had exceeded its powers in the sentence pronounced. Their jurisdictions do not, in general, depend on where the offenses were committed.

Transfers, Demotions, Separation, Resignation

Changes are bound to happen within an organization concerning its structure, functions, and workload. These changes affect the number and types of jobs that are to be staffed within the organization. Similarly, changes occur within the human resource of an organization, in terms of qualifications, capacities, attitudes, and behavior.

All these changes necessitate changes in the placement of the human resource using transfers, promotion, demotions, and sometimes even layoffs. This movement is a function of placement, defined as the assignment of the right man to the right job.

Job requirements continually charge to meet the operational needs of certain departments and management must be able to meet the required changes in the qualifications of employees to make full use of the employees' talents, provide changes for employees' advancement and growth, boost employee morale, and upgraded employee relations.

Changes in human resource status should be compatible with organizational objectives and the welfare of its human resource.

According to Stoner, 1989, the movement of personnel with an organization - their promotion, transfer, demotion, and separation is a major aspect of human resource management. The actual decisions about whom to promote and whom to fire can also be among the most difficult and most important a manager has to make,

Most managers proceed on the general valid assumption that most employees want to qualify for better jobs in the course of their work lives. Promotion, however, is not the only personnel decisions which concern managers and employees. Transfers and layoffs are also ways in which the changing fortunes of the organization are adjusted to human resources.

Transfer

A transfer is the reassignment of an employee to a job with similar pay, status, duties, and responsibilities (Carrell, Kuzmits, Elbert, 1989). A transfer of an employee may occur within the same department or unit in a firm where the employee is moved from one job to another of equivalent rank or the same pay class within the firm (Sison, 1991).

Kinds of Transfers

Temporary - When an employee is transferred temporarily to another job created by vacation or sick leaves, he has an opportunity to show his versatility and expand his knowledge and ability.

Permanent - while the transferee has the opportunity, he must prove his worth by consistent development of his skills in coping with the present trends, particularly in matters of leadership.

Types of Transfers may be grouped into:

Production transfer. This is intended to avoid layoffs on the job while workers are being hired for a similar type of work elsewhere.

Replacement Transfer. The intention is similar to that of production transfer. However, the employee with a long service record is transferred to a similar job in another department where he replaces another with a shorter service record.

Versatility Transfer. This is intended to train workers to handle a variety of jobs in preparation for production or replacement transfers or small companies.

Shift Transfer. When shift assignments do not rotate, transfers are made from a less favorable shift to a more favorable shift.

Remedial Transfer. This is intended to correct the faulty selection or placement of an employee.

Demotion

Demotion is the movement of an employee from one job to another of a lower rating, lower employment status, or lower rank. Demotion need not involve a reduction in pay. Some companies demote employees without reducing their pay (Sison, 1991).

It is the reassignment of an employee to a lower job with less pay, involving fewer skills and responsibilities. Demotions may take place for reasons beyond the control of the employees.

Reasons for Demotion

Failure of the employee either to qualify for work on the occupational level to which he has been assigned or to meet established job standards.

As a form of disciplinary or punitive action against an employee found guilty of violating company policies or rules. Such action is seldom resorted to in most business concerns because it lowers morale and can hurt the employee's performance.

The inability of the employee to meet the requirements of the job due to age, poor health, or physical disability.

Reduction in business so that the number of positions at certain levels must be reduced, or elimination of certain functions requiring a reduction in manpower. This demotion is not due to the fault of the employee.

Many managers and personnel administrators agree that demotion is not an effective way to handle the disciplinary problem. Demotion will not improve the behavior of an employee who has a long record of poor work habits, such as chronic absenteeism, insubordination, or drinking on the job. Those problems are most likely to be remedied by supervisory counseling, corrective discipline, and employee rehabilitation.

In some situations, involving unsatisfactory performance, employees may be the recipients of a rather common aberration of personnel management: the promotion-demotion. Here, employees are "kicked upstairs" to higher "paying jobs which typically involve little authority or responsibility.

Demotion-promotion is a common way of dealing with a loyal long-term employee (generally near retirement) who has become obsolete or untrainable in the job. A more meaningful and equitable approach would be to keep the employee in the present job but reassign a portion of the authority and responsibilities to others.

As a general rule demotion should be cautiously resorted to for it badly affects individual and group morale and productivity. The alternative to demotion should be retraining or re-orientation on the job and attitude toward work or termination of employment if no improvement is achieved.

Separation

Human resources management is a very critical task of the human resource department (HRD) wherein they play a great role in coming up with a well-selected employee leading to effective and efficient production in the organization. But the staffing process doesn't end with recruiting and selecting employees but they continue the process of training and development evaluation, changes of personnel status, and finally to a separation of an employee. Some may be separated through voluntary or involuntary due to some reason.

Separation is the termination of employment as a result of retirement, resignation, dismissal. Lay-off or dropping from the rolls. It is the termination of either temporary or permanent which is initiated by the employee or the employees (Milkovich, G. & Boudreau, J. 1994). Separation is costly where the agency needs funds to advertise vacancies, selection, training and development.

Voluntary separation is better known as resignation or quit. This termination of employment is generally initiated by the employee.

Causes of Voluntary Resignation

Dissatisfaction about wages and working conditions, misunderstandings with supervisors or fellow-workers, and inconvenient work hours are among the chief reasons for employee resignation.

In many cases, an employee leaves the company to accept a better job is another organization where the rate of pay is higher, the personnel policies are better, promotional opportunities are greater, or the working conditions in general opportunities are great, or the working conditions, in general, are more agreeable to the employee.

Other reasons are personal, such as family circumstances, physical and health conditions, and a desire to continue one's studies. In case of voluntary resignation, Philippine laws do not provide for any separation pay.

The five (5) modes of separation that commonly are practiced in the Philippines setting are retirement, resignation, dismissal, lay-off, and dropping from the rolls.

Modes of Separation
A. Retirement

It is the separation the termination from the job with a minimum of 15 years of permanent service and is a result of a choice process.

1. Kinds of retirement

   a. Mandatory retirement. It is the termination of employment due to old age which is 65 years old
   b. Optional retirement. Termination of an employee due to some reasons; lower than 65 years of age but at least rendered 15 years in service with a permanent position.

2. Five Categories of retirement

   a. As soon as finally feasible
   b. Compulsory retirement and willingness to take it
   c. Compulsory retirement but reluctance to take it
   d. Retirement following and due to health and unemployment

e. Retirement due to health and other problems

3. Reasons for early retirement

   a. Health Conditions. This involves poor sight, poor hearing, and poor physical mobility.
   b. Mental Health. Poor concentration, poor psychomotor skills.
   c. Knowledge Requirement. Obsolete knowledge & no updates.
   d. Job Satisfactions - Unmotivated employee tends to retire early.

4. Advantages of Early Retirement (Omnibus Rules, 1997)

   a. On the part of the employee
       1. Cash lump sum
       2. Life monthly pension at the age after 65 yrs.
   b. On the part of the agency - cost reduction

5. Disadvantages of Early Retirement

   a. On the part of the employee
       1. cash lump sum is lesser against his compulsory retirement
       2. the monthly pension is lesser
   b. On the part of the organization - loss of valuable and experienced workers who contribute much to the former employee.

B. Resignation

It is a voluntary written notice of an employee informing the appointing authority that he is relinquishing his positions and stating the date such as resignation shall take effect. The acceptance of resignation in writing by the agency or the appointing authority should be submitted to the CSC for record purposes. (Omnibus Rules, 1995).

Factors Causing resignation

   a. Individual characteristics factors
   b. Labor market factors
   c. Scope of organization factors

C. Lay-Off

Causes of lay-off due to economic reasons that cannot be controlled by the organizations:

   a. Poor business decisions
   b. Poorly designed products

It would be advisable to have the following policies regarding lay-offs:

Advance commitment regarding laying off will cushion the shock of lay off. Under the straight seniority policy, the last employee laid off is the first one recalled.

Permanent layoffs should be planned as far in advance as possible. At least one week's advance notice of lay off should be given and a longer notice to long-service employees.

Management should consider the possibility or compensation for permanent displacements caused by technological change, shutting down less, efficient plants, etc. The amount of compensation should vary with the employee's earnings and length of service.

Management should take an effort to place laid-off employees with other firms in the community. It can work with agencies in the labor market that are seeking to place workers in new jobs.

Management should train workers to do several jobs so that they can be transferred rather than laid off.

D. Dismissal

Involuntary termination of employment that is initiated by the employer. Dismissal is executory only after the confirmation by the department secretary's concern (CSC module 4).

1. Reasons for Dismissal (Milkovich and Boudreau, 1994)

High rates of discharge are due to selection errors.

   a. Harmful behavior
   b. Poor performance -from PES
   c. Sexual harassment
   d. Habitual absenteeism & tardiness
   e. Nepotism

Exemptions, teachers, AFP, & employee on a confidential capacity

2. Implication of Dismissal

Quality remaining employees may lose trust in the organization and consider withdrawal behaviors (Milkovich, & Boudreau, J. 1994)

E. Dropping from the Roll (Omnibus Rules, 1995)
    Causes of dropping from the rolls

   (1) AWOL
       An officer or employee who is absent for at least 30 days without approved leave is considered absent without leave. If the number of authorized absences incurred is less than 30 calendar days; a written return to work order shall be served on the official or employee at his last known address on record. Failure to report for work within the period stated in the order shall be a valid ground to drop from the rolls.

(2) Unsatisfactory or Poor performance.
1. Two consecutive unsatisfactory ratings may cause an employee to be dropped from the rolls after due notice.
2. Notice shall be given not later than 30 days from the end of the semester that enable the former employee to explain.
3. One poor performance evaluation rating will be dropped after due notice.

(3) Physical and mental unfitness
1. Absent for more than one year due to illness when declared physically unfit.
2. Intermittently absent because of illness for at least 260 working days during 24 months period may be declared physically unfit.
3. An employee who is behaving abnormally for an extended period of mental disorder and incapacity to work as reported by co-workers or supervisors, or confirmed by the head may likewise drop from the rolls.
4. An employee who received a notice of dropped from the rolls has the right to appeal within 15 days after receipt of the notice.
5. Dropping from the rolls is not disciplinary and shall not result in forfeiture of any benefits on the part of the official nor disqualifying him from employment in the government (Omnibus Rules, 1995).

Exit Interview

The exit interview is an attempt to find out from an employee the actual reasons for his quitting the present organization. It is a device for discovering vital information about the company's policies or practices and its employee relations program and is intended to ascertain the employee's reactions to various facets of his work, such as dissatisfaction with any aspect of his job or the working conditions, or his relationship with fellow employees or his supervisors.

The exit interview is conducted for the following purposes:

1. To ascertain from the employee the real reasons for his leaving the present job.
2. To give the employee an indication of his future career in the company, to dissuade him from quitting if he is a desirable employee.
3. To create goodwill towards the company.
4. To check whether he has accomplished all papers and clearances to make sure that he received all that is due him from the Social Security System and the company.

The exit interview is a means of identifying the sore spots in the organization and the possible shortcomings of management so that the necessary remedies may be instituted. It is also one way of knowing the ills such as personality conflicts, that exist in the company or in the department where the employee has been working.

Guidelines for Dismissing Employees

DO's	DON'Ts
Give many warnings as possible for mass layoffs. Sit down one-on-one with the individual, in a private office.	Don't leave room for confusion when firing. Tell individuals in the first sentence they are terminated.
Complete a firing session within 15 minutes.	Don't allow time for debate during a firing session.
Provide written explanations of severance benefits.	Don't make personal comments when firing someone.
Provide outplacement services away from company Headquarters.	Don't rush a fired employee off-site unless security is an issue.
Be sure the employee hears about the termination from a manager, not a colleague.	Don't fire people on significant dates, like the 25th Anniversary of their employment or the day their mother died.
Express appreciation for what the employee has Contributed, if appropriate.	Don't fire employees when they are on vacation or Have just returned.

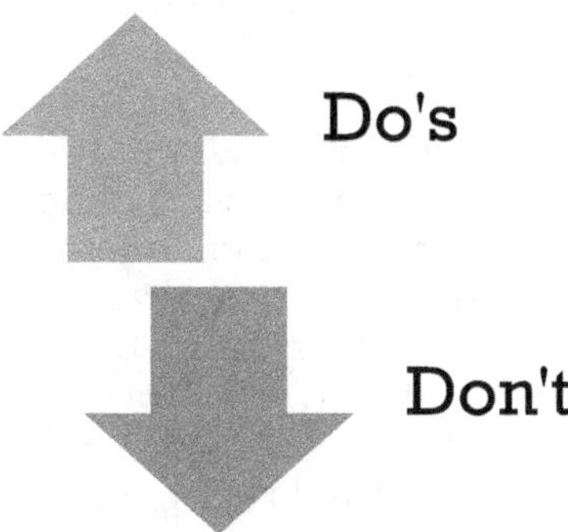

Retirement of AFP Personnel

The pertinent law which establishes the system of retirement and separation for military personnel of the Armed Forces of the Philippines is Presidential Decree NO. 1650.

For purposes of this Decree, active service of a military person shall mean active service rendered by him as a commissioned officer, enlisted man, cadet, probationary officer, trainee or draftee in the Armed Forces of the Philippines and service rendered by him as a civilian official or employee in the Philippine Government before the date of his separation or retirement from the Armed Forces of the Philippines, for which military and/or civilian service he shall have received payment from the Philippine government, and/or such others as may hereafter be prescribed by law as active service; Provided, that for purposes of retirement, he shall have rendered at least ten (10) years of active service as an officer or enlisted man in the Armed Forces of the Philippines: and Provided further, that no period of such civilian government service longer than his active military service shall be credited for purposes of retirement.

Upon attaining fifty-six (56) years of age or upon accumulation of thirty (30) years of satisfactory active service, whichever is later, an officer or enlisted man shall be compulsorily retired; Provided; that such officer or enlisted man who shall have attained fifty-six 56 years of age with at least twenty (20) years of active service shall be allowed to complete thirty (30) years of service but not beyond his sixtieth (60th) birthday; provided, however, that such military personnel compulsorily retiring by age shall have at least twenty (20) years of active service; Provided, further, that the compulsory retirement of an officer serving in a statutory position shall be rendered until completion of the tour of duty prescribed by law and, provide, finally, that the active service of military personnel may be extended by the President if, in his opinion, such continued military service is for the good of the service.

Notwithstanding the provisions of Sec. 5 (a), military personnel in the active service, who otherwise will retire compulsorily under Section 1 (b) of Republic Act Numbered Three Hundred Forty, as amended, during the first, second, third, fourth, fifth and sixth calendar years of the effectivity of this Decree, shall be retired compulsorily under this Decree on the dates they shall complete on the additional period of service of one, two, three, four, five, and six years, respectively. Provided that such additional period of service shall not extend beyond that fifty sixths (56th) birthday or completing of thirty (30) years of active service, whichever is later: Provided, further that such military personnel who have attained fifty-six (56) years of age but have not completed thirty (30) years of active service on the effectivity of the Decrees shall be allowed complete thirty (30) years of active service but not beyond their sixtieth (60th) birthday; Provided, finally, that such military personnel should have completed at least fifteen years of active service."

Resignation and Reversion of Regular and Reserve Officers
 A. Resignation. This is a method of voluntarily leaving the military service and enjoyed by officers, both reserve and regular. Resignation can easily be affected provided the officer has no contractual obligation with the government. Otherwise, he shall be required to pay back the government. Resignations are coursed to the Office of the President thru channels. The President's approval serves as a basis for the issuance of orders.
 B. Reversion. RA 2334 provides that reserve officers shall be rotated in the active military service for the primary purpose of making available for the service in the event of an emergency, the maximum, number of trained and qualified reserve officers. By these objectives, commanders concerned should consider the active duty of a reserve officer primarily to train him for his projected utilization in case of need.
 C. Reserve officers, on the other hand, should not look upon active military service as a career but rather a means of discharging their military obligation under the Constitution and NDA. Continuing turn-over of reserve officers' incident to the rotation should not prejudice the operational effectiveness of units/services. Rotation of reserve officers must be premised on the realization of the long-term objectives of the NDA, which is the strengthening and effectiveness of AFP units. Below are details for implementing the scheme.
   (a) Implementation of RA 2334 is decentralized to Major Services. GHQ & AFPWSSUs are considered as one Major Service.
   (b) Reversion shall be covered by orders. Such orders issued and effected shall remain in force unless nullified for want of authority of fraudulent issuance.
   (c) The number of officers in each Major Service to be reverted during the fiscal year shall be determined by Major Service Commander's base upon authorized troop ceilings for the fiscal year and needs of the service consistent with the objective of rotation under existing laws.

 D. Discharge

   Discharge is a form of separation from the service which is administrative and distinguished from a statutory one. Officers and enlisted personnel alike may be discharged administratively. Regular and Reserve Officers on an extended tour of active duty for 6 months or more shall be administratively discharged from the service only upon approval of the President. Officers and EP may be administratively discharged due to the following circumstances.
   Physical disability and/or separation due to the officer's misconduct, willful failure to perform his/her duties, intemperate use of drugs or alcoholic liquor, or vicious or immoral habits;

Physical disability not due to the officer's misconduct, willful failure to perform his or her duties, intemperate use of drugs of alcoholic liquor, vicious or immoral habits.

Separation not due to the officer's misconduct, willful failure to perform his/her duties, intemperate use of drugs or alcoholic liquor, vicious or immoral habits. An AFP Board of Review shall be established and shall consist of not less than 5 or more than 7 members to be appointed by DND. One member shall be from the JAGS. Where physical fitness of an officer is an issue, at least one member shall come from the Major Service of respondent officer for discharge after trial by court-martial, is determined to be more convenient, practical and expeditious, consistent with the requirements of discipline, morale, and welfare and the interest of the service.

For the good of the service.

Unsuitability - Not due to misconduct but to ineptitude or ineptness due to lack of general adaptability, want to readiness or inability to learn, character and behavior disorders, personality disorders due to psychiatric conditions, chronic alcoholism, or addiction, homosexual tendencies.

Cases Subject to Review
Those in which an Efficiency and Separation Board. (ESB) has recommended the discharge of an officer.
Those in which the proper commander does not concur with the recommendation of an ESB for the retention of an officer.
Those involving the compulsory separation of officers for the failure of promotion.

Labor-Management Relations
As a registered nurse at Kaiser Permanente and a member of the California Nurses Organization, the biggest union in the entire United States of America with 19,000 members, I observed and experienced how labor-management relations work. CNA and KP have a master agreement which covers all Registered Nurses who are employed in the existing facilities of the Employer located in Northern California. Our agreement has preamble to promote optimal patient outcomes and to adhere to applicable state and federal statutes related to the delivery of health care.
The KP-CNA agreement declares: "The parties agree that competent performance of the essential functions of bargaining unit direct care Registered Nurses (RNs) and Nurse Practitioners (NPs) as determined by Registered nursing and hospital licensing law and regulations, requires the application of scientific knowledge and technical skill in the physical, social and biological sciences and the exercise of independent, discretionary judgment by direct care RN/NP in the interest of the assigned patient."
Unions are an organization that employees designate to represent them collectively in bargaining with the employer for wages and other conditions of employment. The objectives of a union include obtaining improved wages and

other employment conditions in the labor contract, increasing membership, and administrating the contract. The labor contract is a written agreement negotiated between management and the union that governs the conditions of employment. The various reasons for and methods of unionization, and union-related objectives and activities, are referred to as the labor relations process (Drummond, 1990).

Labor Union

A labor union is an employee organization formed primarily to negotiate employment contracts on behalf of its members, using the process known as collective bargaining. Collective bargaining addresses various employee concerns, including wages, benefits, and working conditions. Labor unions provide other services to their members as well, such as insurance and pension plans, and they represent their members in disputes with employers (Pope, et. al., 1995).

Legal Authority

Although workers in the United States have organized for generations, the union movement was given a significant boost in the 1930s, when Congress passed the National Labor Relations Act (NLRA). This act, known as the Wagner Act, gave the union the legal authority to represent groups of workers – called bargaining units – in the collective-bargaining process. These units consist of groups of employees whose places of work, employers, or job tasks give them a common interest in such work-related issues as pay, working hours, working conditions, vacations, and health benefits.

Not all employees are covered by NLRA. For example, management employees, government workers, and farm and household workers are not covered, but their right to bargain collectively may be covered by other laws.

The NLRA also created a federal agency, the National Labor Relations Board (NLRB), to be responsible for supervising and regulating the negotiating process between employers and unions. Federal labor laws enacted after NLRA provide that collective-bargaining agreement are enforceable in court and establish procedures to assure that union leaders represent the interest of their members (Pope, et. al., 1995)

Types of Unions

In her book, Human Resources Management for the Hospitality Industry, Karen Drummond wrote: "There are three types of unions: international, national, and local. National labor unions have membership solely within the United States. When its membership is from both within and outside the United States, it is referred to as an international union. Local unions represent employees in a limited geographic area, and they constitute the greatest number of unions in the United States. Most local unions are affiliated and operate under the constitution of a national or international union. The local union is run by elected officials who carry out the daily union operations."

Important Union Terms

Collective bargaining is the process by which the labor contract between the union and management is negotiated and enforced. A bargaining unit is a group of two or more employees who share common employment interests and conditions and can be reasonably grouped for collective bargaining purposes. Union contracts define the bargaining unit – in other words, who can join and be represented by the union. The union steward is an employee designated by the union to check on contract compliance and advise employees of their rights and what the union is doing for them. They are trained to identify and negotiate grievances (Drummond,1990).

Why Managers Resist Union

According to Drummond managers frequently voice complaints about unions and use techniques to avoid unionization. Why? They are concerned that unionization will create conflict between employees who support the union and those who reject it. They are also concerned that it may cause lowered employee commitment and productivity, loss of direct communication between employees and management, and increased payroll costs. Additionally, managers may feel some of their rights, such as giving promotions and rewards, will be subject to union rules and endorsement.

Organizing A Union

The first step in the union organizing of employees is to make contact with them and find out about their complaints and needs. This may be in response to unhappy employees who have contacted the union. In this way, the union starts to build a case for itself as its representative in dealing with the employer. The union also tries to determine how vulnerable the employer is. An employer that allows on-premises solicitation by any outside groups or charities, must also let union organizers solicit employees, although this is permitted only in noncustomer, nonwork areas during break periods. If the organizer cannot get on the premises to talk to employees because of a no-solicitation rule, they will commonly talk to employees in or close to parking lots and at workers' homes and hangouts (Drummond, 1990).

When must an employee join a union to get or keep a job? When the majority of workers have voted to belong to a union per rules and regulations of the National Labor Relations Board and similar agencies. An employee cannot refuse to join a union that is legally authorized to represent his co-workers except in those states which have right-to-work laws (Hanna, 1974).

Right-to-Work laws

In their book, Legal Problem Solver, John A. Pope, Jr., et al., wrote: "When you start a new job, you may be faced with the question of whether or not to join a union. In some states and for some jobs, the decision may already have been made for you. Because of an agreement between an employer and the union, you may be automatically added to the union's rolls. But in more than 20 states, you make the decision. These states have enacted right-to-work laws, which prohibits employers from requiring union membership as a condition of getting or holding a job."

Grievance Procedure

A grievance procedure is a formal means for handling complaints and problems in the workplace. Most labor unions have negotiated grievance procedures as part of their master agreement, whereby the union steward or other intermediary transmits workers' complaints to management. The purpose of these procedures is to bring order to the workplace, promote communication, and minimize or prevent labor disputes (Pope, et. al., 1995).

Industrial Relations

In the online magazine "Navigator", author Rakha R defines industrial relations as the relations and interactions in the industry particularly between the labor and management as a result of their composite attitudes and approaches regarding the management of the affairs of the industry, for the betterment of not only the management and the workers but also of the industry and the economy as a whole.

The term "Industrial Relations" comprises of "Industry" and "relations". Industry means any productive activity in which an individual is engaged. It includes – (a) primary activities like agriculture, fisheries, plantations, forestry, horticulture, mining, etc. etc. and (b) secondary activities like manufacturing, construction, trade, transport, commerce, banking, communication, etc.

Economically speaking, industry means the secondary sector where factors of production (land, labor, capital, and enterprise or four M's – men, materials, money, and machines) are gainfully employed for production, and where a business organization exists.

"Relations' means the relations that exist in the industry between the employer and his workforce.

Scope of Industrial Relations

The scope of industrial relations includes:

> (a) Relationships among employees, between employees and their supervisors or managers.
> (b) Collective relations between trade unions and management. It is called union-management relations.
> (c) Collective relations among trade unions, employers' associations, and government.

Objectives of Industrial Relations

The two-fold objectives of good industrial relations are to preserve industry peace and to secure industrial cooperation.

Three Main Participants in Industrial Unit

> 1. The workers and their unions,
> 2. Employees and their associations, and

3. Government

Changing Trends in Labor-Management Relations

Economic liberalization and globalization have had a tremendous impact on labor-management relations.

Economic Liberalization – the Indian economy, which was liberalized in the year 1991, shifted its focus from import substitutions to export promotion and domestic competition. Thus, domestic firms had to compete with multinational firms.

Globalization – is defined as the growing liberalization of international trade and investment, due to the integration of national economies. Most workers associate globalization with the loss of jobs. They strongly feel that globalization has always hurt labor relations.

Trust and Cooperation

Trust and cooperation are essential in labor relations. They help build a partnership between workers and employers and both groups to work together. Lack of trust and cooperation between the two groups can result in conflicts, disputes, and strikes. That slows down the productivity of the organization (Rakha R).

Laws, Regulations and Court Decisions Related to HRM

Major Federal Laws and Regulations Related to Human Resources Management (Robbins, 1988)

Year	Law or Regulation	Description
1963	Equal Pay Act	Prohibits pay differences based on sex for equal work
1964 (amended in 1972)	Civil Rights Act, Title VII	Prohibits age discrimination based on race, color, religion, national origin, or sex
1967 (as amended)	Age Discrimination in Employment Act	Prohibits age discrimination against employees between 40 and 65 years of age
1973	Vocational Rehabilitation Act	Prohibits discrimination based on physical or mental handicaps
1974	Veterans' Readjustment Act	Prohibits discrimination against disabled veterans and Vietnam War veterans
1974	Privacy Act	Gives employees the legal right to examine letters of reference concerning them

1978	Pregnancy Discrimination Act, Title VII	Prohibits the dismissal of women because of pregnancy alone and protects job security during maternity leaves
1978	Mandatory Retirement Act	Prohibits the forced retirement of most employees before the age of 70

Major Supreme Court Decisions on Employment (Robbins, 1988)

Year	Case	Ruling
1984	Fire Fighters' Local (Tennessee) vs. Stotts	Layoffs of Memphis firefighters must go by seniority unless there are black employees who can show they are victims of racial bias.
1986	Wygant vs. Jackson (Michigan) Board of Education	Layoffs of white employees to maintain racial or ethnic ratios are illegal, but affirmative action plans that sot whites' entry-level jobs were endorsed.
1986	Fire Fighters' Local (Ohio) vs. City of Cleveland	Affirmative action plans with numerical guidelines may be used to promote minority members who are not themselves the victim of bias.
1987	U.S. vs. Paradise (Alabama)	Racial quotas may be used to promote minority members where there is evidence of serious racial discrimination.
1987	Johnson vs. Transportation Agency	Affirmative action plans may be used to correct a manifest imbalance in an organization's workforce as long as the rights of others are not unnecessarily trammeled.

Chapter VI

MAINTENANCE: Health, Safety, and Security

Health is wealth. Working employees as well as employers need to keep themselves at the pink of health. Good health brings a positive outlook on life and is productive. Health is vital to employment. Most of the companies offer health insurance to the employees as part of the benefits. This benefit includes medical, dental, and vision.

As employers have come to realize that the well-being of their employees contributes strongly to company productivity, they have adopted programs for helping employees with their problems. One of these is the employee assistance program, or EAP, now offered by many larger employers and a growing number of smaller ones. The typical EAP helps employees get assistance for personal, medical, legal, and other problems (Pope, 1995)

Health and Life Insurance

In his book "Human Resources Management for the Hospitality Industry" Keren Eich Drummond explains the importance of health and life insurance. Here is what she wrote:

Health insurance is the most common benefit in the U.S. In 1983, the most expensive benefit for employers to pay was Social Security pay for retirement. In 1988, health insurance became the most expensive benefit, largely because health care costs have been increasing dramatically since 1956. One result of this has been that more organizations are shifting part of the cost of health insurance onto the employees. By far a majority of employers in the United States offer health insurance to their employees.

Drummond further said that more and more employers are offering a health maintenance organization (HMO) or preferred provider organization (PPO) option. An HMO is an organization of physicians and other healthcare professionals who provide all services to employees enrolled voluntarily under a prepaid plan. Some HMOs may require a minimal copayment of, for example, two dollars when an enrollee uses services. Plan members must use HMO-approved physicians and hospitals. Often the HMO has its building in which its health services are provided. HMOs emphasized preventive care, in part to provide care early and keep the cost down. PPOs came about, as did HMOs, due to the spiraling costs of healthcare; both have helped contain costs. PPOs may be either a hospital or a group of physicians offering a plan to provide all medical services for employees using those facilities. Employers usually encourage employees to use the PPO be covering much more of their expenses if they do.

As a general rule, the larger the employer, the greater the number of supplemental health benefits available. From most to least popular, these benefits include detailed plans, prescription drug plans, and vision care plans.

Drummond concluded that the most prevalent life insurance plan is a group term life insurance. The most popular benefits in case of death or disability are accident death and disability (AD&D) and long-term disability (LTD) insurance.

Maslow's Hierarchy of Needs

According to Abraham Maslow in his hierarchy of needs, safety, and security land next to physiological needs which underscores the order of importance. Everyone needs a secure safe environment to thrive in the work environment. The role of HRM is to make sure the safety of everybody working inside and outside the organization.

In his book, Management, Ricky W. Griffin explains that Abraham Maslow, a human relationist, argued that people are motivated to satisfy five need levels. At the bottom of the hierarchy are the physiological needs – things like food, sex, and air that represent basic issues of survival and biological function. In organizations, these needs are generally satisfied by adequate wages and the work environment itself, which provides restrooms, adequate lighting, comfortable temperatures, and ventilation.

Next are the security needs for a secure physical and emotional environment. Examples include the desire for housing and clothing and the need to be free from worry about money and job security. These needs can be satisfied in the workplace by job continuity (no layoffs), a grievance system (to protect against arbitrary supervisory actions), and an adequate insurance and retirement benefits package (for security against illness and provision of income in later life). Even today, however, depressed industries and economic decline can put people out of work and restore the primacy of security needs.

Belongingness needs to relate to the social process. They include the need for love and affection and the need to be accepted by one's peers. These needs are satisfied for most people by family and community relationships outside of work and friendships on the job. A manager can help satisfy these needs by allowing social interaction and making employees feel like part of a team or workgroup.

Esteem needs comprise two different sets of needs: the for positive self-image and self-respect and the need for recognition and respect from others. A manager can help address these needs by providing a variety of extrinsic symbols of accomplishment such as job titles, nice offices, and similar rewards as appropriate. At a more intrinsic level, the manager can provide challenging job assignments and opportunities for the employee to feel a sense of accomplishment.

At the top of the hierarchy are the self-actualization needs. These involve realizing one's potential for continued growth and individual development. The self-actualization needs are perhaps the most difficult for a manager to address. It can be argued that these needs must be met entirely from within the individual. But a manager can help by promoting a culture wherein self-actualization is possible. For instance, a manager could give employees a chance to participate in making decisions about their work and the opportunity to learn new things about their jobs and the organization.

In 1943, Abraham Maslow advanced a theory suggesting that people are motivated by a hierarchy of needs, including monetary incentives and social acceptance (Griffin, 1996).

Maslow's Hierarchy of Needs Chart

Chapter VII

RECORDS, AUDITS, AND RESEARCH

The objectives of records, audit, and research are to develop a good system of record-keeping, formulate a checklist for carrying out annual personnel audit, carry out research on various subjects of interest to the organization, and make contracts with professional management organizations which serve as a source of research material (Chand, 2020).

Financial Records

Keeping financial records is a necessary chore, but it is often difficult to know which documents to keep and for how long. The following guidelines are designed to help you put your financial records in order and keep them that way (Pope, 1995).

Tax Records

Because you must document your income for the Internal Revenue Service (IRS), keep a home file containing the W-2 and 1099 forms that report income. If you itemize deductions (or if there is a chance that you will), save all records of potential deductions, such as medical expenses, interest payments on your mortgage, charitable contributions, and any business expenses that are not reimbursed by your employer. Because the IRS keeps tax returns on file for seven years, you should do the same, saving copies of your tax returns and all supporting records in the event of an IRS audit. For the same reason, you should also keep your bank statements and your canceled checks for seven years. Store tax-related documents in a safe and accessible place, such as a metal file cabinet.

Other Financial Records

Stock certificates, bonds, deeds, mortgages, and similar documents should be kept in a bank safe-deposit box for extra security. When you buy or sell stocks, bonds, or real estate, but the documents that relate to the sales such as receipts, canceled checks, closing documents, and financial statements in your income tax files, because you will have to report any gains or losses you made on those sales to the IRS.

Keep utility bills only until you receive the subsequent bills, verifying that your accounts are up to date. Of course, if you are having a dispute with the company, keep all the bills until the dispute is resolved.

Inventory of Records

Prepare a list indicating where you have stored important financial records and documents. Tell trusted relatives and friends where they can find the list in case of an emergency.

Aside from doing regular accounting work such as preparing tax returns and auditing, CPAs may examine and report on the financial records of corporations and individuals. Unlike a noncertified accountant, a CPA has a fiduciary relationship (one of trust) with his client and must hold his client's business in strict confidence. For example, if he is hired by the board of directors of a corporation to examine its books, he is responsible for them and not to the management of the corporation. He is also obligated to report erroneous information in financial statements that he reviews (Pope, 1995).

Audits

Audits are an independent appraisal of an organization's accounting, financial, and operational systems. The two major types of financial audits are the external audit and the internal audit (Griffin, 1996).

External audits are financial appraisals conducted by experts who are not employees of the organization. External audits are typically concerned with determining that the organization's accounting procedures and financial statements are compiled in an objective and verifiable fashion. The organization contracts with certified public accountants (CPAs) for this service. The CPA's main objective is to verify for stockholders, the IRS, and other interested parties that the methods by which the organization's financial managers and accountants prepare documents and reports are legal and proper. External audits are so important that publicly held corporations are required by law to have external audits regularly, as an assurance to investors that the financial reports are reliable.

Whereas external audits are conducted by external accountants, an internal audit is handled by employees of the organization. Its objective is the same as that of an external audit – to verify the accuracy of financial and accounting procedures used by the organization. Internal audits also examine the efficiency and appropriateness of financial and accounting procedures. because the staff members who conduct them are a permanent part of the organization, internal audits tend to be more expensive than external audits. But employees, who are more familiar with the organization's practices, may also point out significant aspects of the accounting system besides the technical correctness.

Income Tax Audit

An income tax audit is an official examination of an individual or corporate financial records by the Internal Revenue Service (IRS) to determine the accuracy of a tax return. Audits are the primary tool available to the IRS to enforce compliance with tax laws. If an audit reveals that you have taken some improper deductions, for instance, you may owe the IRS extra taxes, interest, and often a penalty as well. The IRS can do an audit within three years of a return being filled, but in specific circumstances, such as fraud, the time limit is seven years. Most audits are made within 18 months of filing a return (Pope, 1995).

Who can be Audited?

Approximately one out of every 100 tax returns are audited, but there is a greater likelihood that some taxpayers will be audited than others. In particular, someone who has a large income or is self-employed may be subject to an audit. Often taxpayers who are to be audited are chosen by the IRS computer program that is designed to identify anything unusual in a tax return. For example, your return may be audited for one of the following reasons:

Tax deductions (such as those for charitable contributions) that are disproportionate to your income.

Failure to provide the appropriate information about certain expenses.

Unusual expenses (such as large travel expenditures for a shoe-repair business).

Income varies widely from year to year.

W-2 forms that do not match those that the IRS has received from your employer.

Also, the Taxpayer Compliance Measurement Program randomly selects approximately 50,000 taxpayers each year and asks them to document every item in their tax returns – a particularly strict type of audit.

Preparing for an Audit

If you get an audit notice in the mail, do not panic – a notice does not always mean you have done something wrong. The IRS may have seen something unusual on your tax return.

Read the audit notice carefully; it may be a simple request for you to send additional documents to the IRS. Most audit notices specifically state the reason for the audit. Suppose you made very large charitable contributions in proportion to your income. The IRS might ask for proof that you made the contributions. Once you send sufficient documentation (such as canceled checks or receipts) the agency may be satisfied and the audit completed.

In the other situation, you may be asked to call an IRS office and make an appointment for the audit to be conducted in person. The IRS will decide where you will meet. An audit examiner, or auditor, will either meet you at his office or if a "field" audit is called for, he will come to your office or that of your attorney or tax preparer. An auditor is not likely to come to your home unless you operate your business from there, or unless it is inconvenient for you to travel for some reason, such as disability. An IRS office audit is preferable since it prevents the auditor from liking through your records for additional information.

Research

Human Resource Management Research is used to evaluate HR practices and performance. Research is a systematic and scientific process of collecting information, analyzing the information, and drawing conclusions for decision-making. At times the research may be advanced, relying on sophisticated designs and statistics. But whether the information is rigorous or not, the research seeks answers to improve performance. There are two kinds of research – academic and applied. Academic research seeks answers to contribute to the existing body of knowledge. Application-oriented research efforts are called applied research. For evaluating the HR performance applied research is conducted (www.whatishumanresource.com).

There are five kinds of applied research – comparative approach, outside authority approach, statistical approach, compliance approach, and MBO approach.

Comparative Approach. The research team compares its organization (or division) with another organization (or division) to uncover areas of poor performance. This approach commonly is used to compare the results of specific activities or programs. It helps detect areas of needed improvement.

Outside Authority Approach. The research team relies on the expertise of a consultant or published research findings as a standard against which activities or programs are evaluated. The consultant or research findings may help diagnose the causes of problems.

Statistical Approach. From existing records, the research team generates statistical standards against which activities and programs are evaluated. With these mathematical standards, the team may uncover errors while they are still minor.

Compliance Approach. By sampling elements of the human resource information system, the research team looks for deviations from laws and company policies or procedures. Through its fact-finding efforts, the team can determine whether there is compliance with company policies and legal regulations.

MBO Approach. When an MBO approach is applied to the human resource management area, the research team can compare actual results with stated objectives. Areas of poor performance can be detected and reported.

Coverage of HR Research

Research in manpower and human resources covers all those specific areas which are the subject matter of personnel administration. The scope of such research may vary from the very simple to the very complex, or the short and inexpensive to the long and costly. Most studies reveal that the four most dominant areas of research are selection; training and development; attitudes and leadership; and measurement devices (Santana).

The human resource researcher seeks to discover the basic relationship which may lead to improved personnel decision-making in such areas as turnover, absenteeism, compensation levels and structure, job satisfaction, employee morale, assessment of meaningful potential, training effectiveness, grievance handling, labor relations, and collective bargaining.

Human resource research areas are often identified in terms of high or low appearance – selection, opinion measurement, training and development, appraisal, motivation, organizational effectiveness, managerial obsolescence, counseling, and retirement. Managerial selection and development and general employee motivation have generally been identified as the two main human resources areas which are in the greatest need for additional research.

HRM Cases

Denied Proper Military Grade and Academic Rank

On November 23, 2000, Captain Juan Dela Cruz joined the prestigious PMA Corps of Professors with a military-grade of captain and academic rank of assistant professor. Having conferred a master's degree before his appointment in the Corps, he should have been appointed with a military-grade of Major and academic rank of an associate professor based on Executive Order 237 however PMA leadership believed he was too young, at age 30, to be appointed to such grade and rank.

If you are the personnel officer, what would be your action(s) to correct the error?

Carried Away by Emotion

Records show that on or about 151400 Sep 01, the S7 pers together with their CMO Officer, LT EG AY had a party held at a resort in Tigbawan, Pigcawayan, Cotabato.

On or about 2000H, the same date, the subject officer who was already tipsy arrived at their BOQ. MAJ MONCHING, OIC Battalion Commander, and MAJ JUMBO PA were watching TV at the BOQ sala when the subject officer arrived. The subject officer while holding a caliber .45 pistol went inside his room and created unnecessary noise by banging the door in front of his superior officers who were watching TV and while uttering a word, "Nagmamarunung kayo". Further, the subject officer went to the radio room and while thereat shouted to the detailed Sgt of the Guard TSg Tommy and the radio operator SSg Doning. In a loud voice, the subject officer called-up Pfc Boy, and both left the Battalion Hqs.

On 2100H, the subj officer went to the boarding house of Pfc Doming at the back of H38IB and told the latter, "Bong, halika, Iparating mo sa amo mo na si MAJ MONCHING na sasama siya sa operasyon. Kung magsama kami sa operasyon, baka ako and makapatay sa kanya" After which subject officer left. The following day, the subj Officer was confronted by MAJ MONCHING regarding his unruly behavior. The subject officer confided to MAJ MONCHING that he had a family problem and asked for an apology. MAJ MONCHING advised him to set aside his family problems while in the performance of his duties and responsibilities.

When investigated, the subj Officer alleged that he was carried away by his emotion when he created unnecessary noise inside his room. He further reasoned out that his actuation on the night of 15 Sep 01 was not intended to insult his superiors but an expression of ill feelings.

Records further disclosed that subj Officer was the subj of complaint of a certain Ruth of Nuro, Upi, Maguindanao for alleged viol of AW 97 (General Article) of CA 408, as amended for intruding her private dwelling during socials on or about 032100 Sep 99 while he was under the influenced of liquor and blatantly accosted her visitor Mike their village chairman. Subj officer was admonished by CO, 38IB for viol of the abovesaid Article of CA 408.

Being an officer-in-charge, what would be your action (s) to solve the problem?

Physical Injuries

This case pertains to the complaint of a certain Justine of Teneorio, Awang, DOS, Maguindanao against TSg Azom PA of 57IB, 61D, PA for alleged Physical Injuries and Indiscriminate Firing.

Records show that on or about 041530 Nov 2000, a vehicular accident transpired along vicinity Mintex, Awang, Datu Odin Sinsuat, Maguindanao between a motorcycle and an owner type jeep. Complainant upon learning that the two (2) sons of her first cousin were involved rushed to the scene of the incident with her husband MSg Gaday and her nephew Bert purposely to bring them to the hospital for medical treatment. While thereat, she noticed that the driver of the jeep involved was attacked by the bystanders, so, they tried to pacify but to no avail. A moment later, subject EM purposely to stop the attackers of the driver of the jeep from attacking the latter who was known later as his brother-in-law Alfredo of PNP Cotabato City. The complainant cautioned subj EM suddenly appeared, fired his handgun for four (4) times in the air purposely to stop firing his gun but instead the former thrust his handgun to her stomach that prompted her to seek cover from her husband who was about to approach them. The Complainant husband succeeded in persuading subject EM to calm down.

Being an officer-in-charge, what would be your action (s) to solve the problem?

Mauling Incident

This pertains to the complaint of Mr. Lee of Del Pilar, Castillejos, Zambales against Pfc Abby PA of 68IB, 7ID, PA for alleged Frustrated Homicide and Malicious Mischief.

Records show that the complainant initially filed a criminal complaint before the Zambales Provincial Office, PNP against subject EM and seven (7) civilians. The complainant averred that in the afternoon of 02 April 2000 at Sitio Marangla, San Agustin, Iba, Zambales, he was mauled by several persons and was poked with a gun by one who was identified as subject EM, who subsequently fired his handgun twice upward. When he rode on a Calesa with his family and companions to evade further harm, they were stone by Pfc Abby's group resulted in the death of a horse. After such a criminal complaint, a copy of the police report was sent by the Governor of Zambales to CO, 68IB copy furnished SND requesting a further investigation on the matter. When investigated, subject EM denied having participated in the incident. He submitted a copy of the Police Report that indeed he was far away when the incident occurred. Likewise, in the testimonies of seven (7) civilian respondents, they admitted to having mauled the complainant after the latter was left by his companion who lately pointed and fired a handgun to them. The incident cropped up from the quarrel of their children playfully bathing in the river.

Being an officer-in-charge, what would be your action (s) to solve the problem?

Gun Tooting

This pertains to the complaint of Mr. Inosente, of Manggahan, Crossing Bayabas, Toril, Davao City, against Pfc Ico PA, of 73IB, 71D, PA, for alleged violation of Art 285 (Other Light Threats) of the Revised Penal Code.

Records show that on 26 Dec 99, while Complainant and his family were having a picnic at Badak Beach Resort, his child was sideswiped by a bicycle. As a result of the incident, his child suffered bruises. While Complainant and the Resort's Security Guard were helping his child, a drunken man approached them and said: 'Tapsing lang yan" (They are very minor). The complainant was irritated when he heard said words and pushed the said drunken man. Moments later, another drunken man appeared, drew a FA, and pointed it towards the Complainant uttering "Ano iyon, military ako". As a consequence, Complainant filed a case before the Office of the Deputy Ombudsman for the Military and later with the MTC, Davao City, against Pfc Ico for the said acts. However, while the case was in progress, the complainant executed an Affidavit of Desistance stating, among others, that he is no longer interested in the outcome of the case. Thus, the case against resp EP was dismissed by the civil court on 08 Feb 00.

Being an officer-in-charge, what would be your action (s) to solve the problem?

Premature Firing of Cal .50 Machine Gun

This has reference to the case of Pfc Saber PA and Pfc Gucci PA, both of 15LAC, lLABn, LABde, PA, for alleged reckless imprudence resulting in multiple homicides and multiple physical injuries.

Investigation report of HI ID, PA disclosed that Pfc Saber, the gunner, and Pfc Gucci, the driver, of AV SFV 1603 (Corregidor) Simba vehicle, were tasked to escort to elements of 4BB led by 1LT del Pilar PA from their ACP at Bud Datu to reaching the town of Jolo, Sulu, the convoy momentarily made a stop to buy additional supplies. The AV, with the wife of Pfc Gucci inside, and several other EPs riding on top, was parked about ten (10) meters behind an M35 truck with its turret pointing to the latter. While parked, and had a conversation with some EPs on top of the armored vehicle. Minutes later, 1LT del Pilar instructed them to move, however, before it could move, bursts of fire rang out from Cal .50 machine gun mounted on AU which resulted in the death of three (3) EPs and wounding of four (4) others on board the M35 truck. Subj EP averred that said the firing was purely accidental and was caused by a defective SOLENOID-C component of the electrical wiring mechanism of the gun.

The Investigator found Pfc Saber liable for gross negligence while Pfc Gucci PA was found liable for the violation of SO Nr 5, HPA S-99. It was opined that there was no way that the Solenoid C component of the electrical firing mechanism of the AV, be it electrically or manually operated could trigger the premature firing of the said gun. The Solenoid which serves as the safety lever of the firing mechanism. When electrically operated, the gunner has to put on the switch and has to step on the firing mechanism to fire. When manually operated the same need not be switched on but the pedal has to be touched/stepped on the fire.

APM found the existence of probable cause against respondent EPs and recommended referral of their case to the Office of the Provincial Prosecutor of Sulu for appropriate action. On the other hand, Pfc Gucci, the driver of the Simba, violated the SOP Nr 5, HPA, dated 18 Jun 99, for allowing his wife to board the Simba.

Given the gravity of the offense, and considering further that the same is a "service-connected case", recommend that the case be referred to a GCM for trial. The matters are purely military issues and the same will be best appreciated by the military than a civil court.

In view thereof, recommend the designation of a PTIO to conduct the reglementary PTI.

Being an officer-in-charge, what would be your action (s) to solve the problem?

Illicit Relationship

The investigation conducted disclosed that on 10 July 1993, Pfc Ecan PA assigned Charlie Company this unit asked permission from his Commanding Officer to leave purposely to review in preparation for his board examination for Civil Engineering and he was granted From the time he left his station he did not bother to communicate with the Company of his whereabouts or situation. Instead, he prolonged his absence. After giving him considerable days, the unit prompted to mark him AWOL effective 5 September 1993 and subsequently dropped from rolls effective 17 September 2001. Subject EP was not able to pursue his review because of his problem regarding his wife. That he noticed and observed that she was having an illicit relationship with one of the WEENA conductors. To confirm all the vital information that he gathers, he asked permission from his wife as an alibi that he will go to Manila to follow up his commission in the AFP. But the fact was he did not go to Manila but instead conducted surveillance on his wife. That on or about 301930 August 1993 subject EP successfully cornered/caught in the act the two and he was not able to hold his temper that he shot and killed the lover of his wife. By then he did not bother to report his whereabouts and situation to his Commanding Officer because of the crime he committed a warrant for his arrest was already issued. He fled and hid until when he was able to amicably settled the case.

Being an officer-in-charge, what would be your action (s) to solve the problem?

Evasion of Responsibility

This case pertains to the complaint of CPT CUTE PA of 191st MP Bn, HHSG, PA for alleged viol of AW 97 (Misconduct/Evasion of Responsibility) of CA 405, as amended.

Records show that the complainant was previously assigned with 24IB and designated as Battalion RSO. Accordingly, upon his relief from the aforesaid battalion, the subject officer took over his position as Bn RSO eff 01

Nov 99. For refusing to accept officially the property accountability of the unit, CPT CUTE lodged a complaint against the subject officer for misconduct and viol of para 6, Article 12 of par 6-1, Proper Transfer of Unit Property Accountability.

When investigated, the subj officer vehemently denied the allegation imputed against him by the complainant. He alleged that he never refused to accept the property accountability of the aforesaid unit. He reasoned out that being the designated RSO of the unit, he must first account or conduct an inventory of the items before accepting such property as a matter of procedure. That his desire to expedite the inventory was hampered by his physical condition where he was admitted at AFP Medical Center on 25 July 00 and required to undergo follow-up check-up for several months. He was able to report only to his unit on 16 Sep 01, assumed the position as Bn RSO, and started conducting a physical inventory of all issued firearms, and subsequently signed the Memorandum Receipts.

Being an officer-in-charge, what would be your action (s) to solve the problem?

Abandonment and Non-Support

This case pertains to the complaint of Mrs. Rosing of Poblacion Sur, Salcedo, Ilocos Sur against her husband Cpl Rocio PA of 60IN, 7ID, PA for alleged Abandonment and Non-Support.

Records show that complainant and subj EM are legally married and were blessed with two (2) children, namely: Gemma and Gabby.

Mrs. Rocio in her complaint alleged that her husband has been remised of his obligation as the father to his children by not visiting their conjugal home and failure to extend financial support to them since he was reassigned in Davao. She further alleged that her husband has a live-in partner with whom he has a child. That she is appealing that she be granted a monthly Class "E" Allotment in the amount of Five Thousand (P5,000.00) Pesos.

When investigated, subj EM specifically denied the charges of his wife against him. He submitted Xerox copies of the receipts and postal money orders to prove that he is not remiss of his financial obligation to his family. He also denied that charges of immorality against him is purely fabricated and has no basis in fact and law. He admitted that he seldom visits their conjugal home considering the distance of his assignment. That he signified his willingness to extend financial support to his family and even submitted a duly executed Class "E" Allotment in the amount of P2,000.00 in favor of his wife eff Oct 01 subject to an increase of PI,500.00 by Jan 03 upon payment of his obligation with AFPSLAI.

On 17 Sep 01, the complainant submitted an Affidavit of Desistance stating therein that her charges against her husband were merely the product of simple misunderstanding and admitted that she has no personal knowledge regarding the immoral acts of her husband she complained of.

Being an officer-in-charge, what would be your action (s) to solve the problem?

Promised to Marry

This case pertains to the complaint of one Joy of Sta Cruz, Manila against Pfc Tuliska PA of 70IB, 7ID, PA for alleged Breach of Promise to Marry and Non-Support.

Records show that complainant and subj EM are common-law spouses and blessed with child Ade who was born on 19 Mar 2000. The complainant alleged that since 1995, subj EM failed to send financial support to her until she gave birth to a baby girl. Even the child reaches the age of one year. Subj EM never sent support to the child.

When investigated, subj EM vehemently denied having abandoned nor neglected to give support to the complainant as both are living together as husband and wife since 1995, even before his enlistment in the regular force. He said that the reason why he seldom goes home to their conjugal home is the distance of his assignments. Then he is not neglecting his responsibility as a father to his daughter and he is willing to marry the complainant by the year 2002 and will execute a Class "E" Allotment in favor of her daughter for One thousand Pesos (PI,000.00) monthly.

Being an officer-in-charge, what would be your action (s) to solve the problem?

Illegal Structure

This pertains to the complaint of Mr. & Mrs. Mufe of Barangay Militar, Fort Magsaysay, Palayan City, against SSgt Fuga PA, assigned with 7ID, PA, for alleged grave threats.

Records show that sometime in 1993, a lot with an area of 300 square meters located at Purok #11, Barangay Militar, Palayan City was awarded to resp EP by the local officials of said place. Considering that resp EP had no money to build a house, he only fenced the said lot and planted fruit-bearing trees. In 1998, Cpl Laguna, the adjacent neighbor of resp EP, donated the lot of resp EP to his relatives, the Complainants, who erected their residential house therein. When resp EP learned the intrusion of the spouses, he got mad and also constructed a house at the side of the house of the Complainants. Hence, this complaint.

Being an officer-in-charge, what would be your action(s) to solve the problem?

Special Case Alpha: Anti-Graft and Corrupt Practices Act

I, Mr. Philippines, of legal age, married, Filipino, with residence and postal address Fort del Pilar, Baguio City, after being duly sworn to by law, hereby depose and state:

That I am a member of the Corps of Professors of the Philippine Military Academy;

On 26 June, I filed my resignation from the military service. One of the requirements for resignation is to have a Philippine Military Academy command clearance. One of the signatories of the command clearance is Major XYZ, a member of the Corps of Professors, who is the Assistant Chief of Staff for Educational Plans and Programs or MA-5. I needed his signature as MA-5 as a prerequisite for other officers in charge of other offices to sign my clearance and eventually complete the requirements;

On 27 June at around 2:00 pm, I went to the office of Major XYZ and requested him to sign my command clearance. However, he declined to sign it because of my status being a beneficiary of the Faculty Incentive Program (FEP). FTP is funded by the PMA Foundation, Inc. (PMAFI), a private entity. A beneficiary of FIP is entitled to reimbursement of his tuition and miscellaneous fees for graduate or post-graduate study by the PMAFI thru MA-5. Major XYZ did not sign my clearance because according to him, I am "obliged to serve PMA one year for every year of scholarship.";

Major XYZ's view with regards to the contractual service obligation for FIP beneficiary was quite different from the view of Major ABC, former MA-5 who encouraged me to avail of FIP being a military instructor of PMA. Major ABC's view is that a beneficiary of FIP is not obliged to serve nor to reimburse the amount spent by PMAFI during the schooling if a beneficiary chooses to resign from the service or be reassigned to other AFP Units as manifested by the previous FIP beneficiaries who resigned from PMA or were reassigned to other AFP Units. These beneficiaries were not obligated to serve PMA for one year for every year of scholarship nor were required to reimburse the amount paid by PMAFI on their schooling;

I was the first beneficiary in the history of FIP where I was asked to reimburse the expenses paid on schooling. Because Major XYZ and I have different views on the interpretation of contractual service obligation, Major XYZ initiated that SOP 19 and Circular 14, the two governing policies on FIP, be referred to the Office of Staff Judge Advocate (OSJA) for legal interpretation. Major XYZ then told me in a gentleman's agreement that whatever be the result of the OSJA legal interpretation we will abide by it. I agreed;

I wanted to expedite the signing of my clearance, I told Major XYZ that I will just reimburse the amount paid by PMAFI for my post graduate schooling however he did not accept my proposal. Instead he told me to go back to him after a legal interpretation made by OSJA on SOP #19 and Circular # 14;

On 08 July the legal interpretation of the Office of Staff Judge Advocate came back as follows:

1) On Contractual Service Obligation "...Thus, there is no contractual service obligation when the scholar has not graduated from the course." (I have not yet graduated from the course when I filed my resignation from the service).

2) On Cost of Training "...If the Philippine Government or foreign host country did not spend any, then, there is no cost of training. If the training or schooling was taken on a government time, then the cost shall be the pay and allowances received while on training or schooling." (In my case, I did not take government time on my schooling. I went to school after office hours and on Saturdays and Sundays. And the government did not spend any amount because my schooling was sponsored by PMAFI, a private entity).

3) "...Contractual Service Obligation applies only when the scholar has completed his course." (In my case, I have not yet completed my course that time).

4) "...The absence of a contract signed by the parties negates any contractual service obligation." (I did not sign a contract on my schooling. On 05 July 2002 MA-5 senior NCO came to me at my department saying he was instructed by Major XYZ to bring the contract and requested me to sign it for the said schooling but I declined to do it).

5) "...To compel the scholar to render service might violate the constitutional prohibition on involuntary servitude."

On 11 July, I went back to the office of MA-5 hoping that Major XYZ will sign my command clearance because of the result of his initiative to let the SOP 19 and Circular 14 be interpreted legally by the Office of Staff Judge Advocate. However, notwithstanding said interpretation, he still refused to sign it causing much delay in the completion of my clearance. Because I was so desperate to have him sign my clearance and because I wanted my command clearance to be signed as early as possible, I told Major XYZ that I am willing to pay the amount of P42,898.80 so I can complete the requirements for my resignation and eventually I can leave the country and join my wife in the United States who urgently needed my presence. However, Major XYZ told me "...you shouldn't pay...you are not at fault... it's the fault of MA-5 for not having you signed a contract..." Major XYZ even told me to just donate my payment to "Major XYZ Foundation" instead. Major XYZ again told me to come back the following week. This delaying tactic has been repeated several times causing me to have mental anguish and sleepless nights. Because Major XYZ did not accept my proposal, I decided not to pay it anymore.

A week after, I went back to Major XYZ and requested him to sign my clearance but this time he had a change of heart. He said he would not sign it if I would not pay the amount of P42,898.80 which was different from what he said previously. I told him I was very much willing to reimburse the amount of P42,898.80 at the outset when I went to him for his signature but he refused to accept my payment. But this time, he was demanding that I pay it;

On 01 August, upon the advice of Major XYZ, I made a letter appeal addressed to the Chairman, Education and Training Board regarding Obligation on Faculty Incentive Program;

On 29 August, because of the inaction of Major XYZ and the Board, I decided to reimburse the amount of P42.898.80 under protest just to facilitate the signing of Major XYZ on my command clearance;

On 02 October, despite the legal interpretation made by the Office of the Staff Judge Advocate on SOP 19 and Circular 14 dated 08 July 2002, Major XYZ sent me a directive reiterating that I am "...obliged to serve PMA one year for every year or fraction thereof of scholarship, reckoned from the time of completion of scholarship..." This is a clear violation of the constitutional prohibition on involuntary servitude;

Because there were much delay and inaction in the performance of Major XYZ's primary duty and responsibility to sign my clearance, and not to collect money on behalf of PMAFI before signing my clearance, there is a clear violation of Republic Act No. 3019 otherwise known as the Anti-Graft and Corrupt Practices Act and Republic Act 6713.

Section 3 of Republic Act 3019 on corrupt practices of public officers, provides:

"Par 6. Causing any undue injury to any party, including the Government, or giving any private party any unwarranted benefits, advantage or preference in the discharge of his official administrative or judicial functions through manifest, partiality, evident bad faith or gross inexcusable negligence. This provision shall apply to officers and employees of offices or government corporations charged with the grant of licenses or permits or other concessions.

"Par 7. Neglecting or refusing, after due demand or request, without sufficient justification, to act within a reasonable time on any matter pending before him to obtain, directly or indirectly, from any person interested in the matter some pecuniary or material benefit or advantage, or to favor his interest or give undue advantage in favor of or discriminating against, any other interested party.

Section 3, Rule VI of Republic Act 6713, provides:

"Sec 3. In case of a written request, petitions or motions sent, using letters, telegrams, or the like, the official or employee in charge shall act on the same within fifteen (15) working days from the receipt thereof."

If you are the head of the Human Resource Department, what action(s) will you do to resolve the issue base on the abovementioned case?

Special Case Bravo: Charge of Discrimination

On June 26, 2005, GO was hired by Respondent as Registered Nurse. On March 30, 2009, Ms. XYZ, 3rd Floor Department Manager, conducted a meeting with 3rd Floor employees where "Speaking English" is one of the Huddle Topics for the week starting from March 30, 2009, to April 5, 2009, which reads, "Speaking non-English in-patient care areas is still a problem. English only in these areas is mandatory." After the meeting, Ms. XYZ and her assistant nurse managers distributed copies of these huddle topics to employees. Some copies were posted on the bulletin boards on the 3rd floor.

On April 10, 2009, at about 09:30 am, GO's sister, Inday, who is an employee of KP working at the Intensive Care Unit, came and talked to GO in Hiligaynon (a local dialect of the Philippines) in the hallway of 3rd Floor regarding the personal and family-related matter. Ms. XYZ, while inside her office, overheard GO's conversation with GO's sister and stepped out from her office asking, "Who is speaking non-English?" LC, a Certified Nursing Assistant on the 3rd floor, who was walking in the hallway near her office, answered by saying, "It was nurse GO talking to his sister." A few minutes later, Ms. ABC, 3rd Floor Assistant Nurse Manager (ANM), came out from their (ANMs) office and walked towards GO and asked to GO if GO spoke the non-English language. GO told Ms. ABC that GO spoke Filipino dialect to GO's a sister. Ms. ABC then told GO that the official language at KP is English-only. GO asked her to show GO the policy but Ms. ABC told GO that GO should ask Ms. XYZ about it. Ms. ABC then left GO and she went to Ms. XYZ's office.

On April 14, 2009, at about 11:45 am, Ms. ABC, approached GO at 3 West break room and asked to GO if GO was in the lunch break. GO said GO was about to take GO lunch break. She asked to GO with her to the manager's office because Ms. XYZ and GO's union representative were at the office waiting for GO. GO told her that GO was not aware of any scheduled meeting with the manager with GO's union representative on that very day and besides GO was scheduled to take GO's lunch break at that time. Ms. ABC insisted that GO should go with her to the manager's office. GO followed her to the office.

Upon entering the manager's office, GO saw Ms. XYZ and Mr. CNA (nurse representative) sitting on their respective chairs facing each other. GO greeted and asked them what the agenda were. Ms. XYZ started to talk about KP policy on English-only rules saying that it has been one of the topics during monthly staff meetings and shift huddles and that employees are mandated to speak English-only but still several employees are speaking non-English.

GO asked Ms. XYZ when the effective date of English-only rules is and what the penalty is if somebody violates it as required by Title VII of the Civil Rights Act. Ms. XYZ told GO, "You don't have to ask me. Just follow my mandate." She further said to me that GO should have accepted GO was wrong when GO spoke in Filipino to GO's sister and should not question the policy. GO politely explained to Ms. XYZ that GO's conversation with GO's sister did not affect the safety and operation of the organization. At that time of GO's conversation with GO's sister, there was no patient present in the hallway.

On May 12, 2009, Ms. RABC told GO to call GO's union's representative for a meeting with Ms. XYZ. At lunchtime of the same day, GO was able to talk to KC (the association's representative) and informed her of the incident and that GO's manager is asking for a meeting.

The meeting was set for 13 May 2009 at 11:00 am at KP 3rd floor manager's office. Present during the meeting were Ms. XYZ, Ms. ABC, KC, and GO. The meeting was started by Ms. XYZ explaining KP policy on English-only rules which mandates employees to comply. Ms. XYZ then handed to GO a copy of the Interoffice Memorandum dated May 13, 2009, with the subject: Verbal Warning – Speaking Non-English in Patient Care Area. A portion of which states: "You are hereby given a letter of verbal warning for failure to consistently abide by mandated guidelines. You must demonstrate significant improvement in the area identified. Failure to meet this guideline may result in further disciplinary action, up to and including termination."

KC asked Ms. XYZ for a copy of KP's English-only rules but Ms. XYZ said that KP has no written policy on English-only rules. KC then told Ms. XYZ that the union will be grieving this English-only expectation and dispute that it occurred in the patient care area. KC then wrote her comments in the Interoffice Memorandum. After the meeting, KC told GO that GO can file a complaint about this incident to the Equal Employment Opportunity Commission (EEOC).

Respondent's reason for its action was that GO violated the company's English-only rules which were not related to patient care and not related to the safety and operation of the hospital.

GO believe GO have been discriminated against because of GO's National Origin (Filipino) in violation of Title VII of the Civil Rights Act of 1964.

If you are the head of the Human Resource Department, what action(s) will you do to resolve the issue base on the abovementioned case?

References

Books

Abasolo, Pacita A. (1991). <u>Personnel Management. The Efficient Management of Employees.</u> GIC Enterprises Co. Inc., Manila, Philippines.

Bartol, Kathryn M., and Martin, David C (1991). <u>Management</u>. New York: Me Graw-Hill, Inc.

Berry, Leonard L., and Seltman, Kent D. (2008). <u>Management Lessons from Mayo Clinic</u>. The McGraw-Hill Companies. The U.S.A.

Bolton, Trevor (1997). <u>Human Resource Management. An Introduction</u>. Cambridge Massachusetts: Blackwell Publishers Ltd.

Campbell, John, et al. (1970). <u>Managerial Behavior, Performance, and Effectiveness</u>. McGraw-Hill. New York, USA.

Cascio, Wayne F. Managing <u>Human Resources: Reproductivity, Quality of Work Life, Profits</u>, 3rd Ed. New York: Me Graw-Hill, Inc., 1992

Cherrington, David J. (1995). <u>The Management of Human Resources</u>. 4th Edition. Prentice Hall, Inc. Englewood Cliffs, New Jersey.

Clark, Robert (1992). <u>Australian Human Resources Management</u>, 2nd Edition. McGraw Hill Book Co., Australia.

Dessler, Garry. <u>Personnel/Human Resource Management</u>. New Jersey: Prentice Hall, Inc., 1991.

Drummond, Karen Eich (1990). <u>Human Resource Management for the Hospitality Industry</u>. Van Nostrand Reinhold. New York, NY 10003

Ferries, Gerald R., and Rowland, Kendrith M. (1988). <u>Human Resource Management</u>. Allyn and Bacon, Inc. USA.

Foz, Vicente B. (1994). <u>The Labor Code of the Philippines and its Implementing Rules and Regulations. Philippine Law</u>. Gazette, Quezon City, Philippines.

Greenlaw, Paul S. & John P. Khol (1986). <u>Personnel Management-Managing Human Resources</u>. Harper and Row Publishers, Inc. New York, USA.

Griffin, Ricky W. (1996). <u>Management</u>.5th Edition. Houghton Mifflin Company. Boston. MA 02116-3764.

Hanna, John Paul (1974). <u>The Complete Layman's Guide to the Law</u>. Prentice-Hall, Inc., Englewood Cliffs, New Jersey.

Harris, Michael (1997). <u>Human Resource Management. A Practical Approach</u>, The Dryden Press, Harcourt Brace College Publishers. Orlando Florida.

Hellriegel, Don, and Slocum, John W. Jr (1986). <u>Management</u>. 4th Edition. Addison- Wesley Publishing Company, Inc. USA.

Ivancevich, John M., and William G Glueck (1989). <u>Foundations of Personnel. Human Resource Management</u>. Richard D. Irwin, Inc. USA.

Julius, Michael J. (1975). <u>Personnel Management</u>. 8th Edition. Richard D. Irwin, Inc, Illinois, USA. Reprinted by National Bookstore, Inc. Philippines.

Jeffres, Robert (1992). <u>Choose Your Attitudes, Change Your Life</u>. SP Publications Inc., USA.

Klatt, Laurence, et. al. (1985). <u>Human Resources Management</u>. Charles E Merrill Publishing Company. Columbus, Ohio.

Koontz, H., and Heinz (1994). Wuterich. <u>Management: A Global Perspective</u>. 10th Edition. Me Graw Hill, Inc.

Kuzmits, Frank E. (1982). <u>Human Resource Management</u>. Merrill Publishing Company. Ohio, USA.

McCormick, Ernest J., and Daniel Ilgen (1980). <u>Industrial Psychology</u>. Prentice-Hall. Englewood Cliffs, New Jersey, USA.

Milkovich, G., and Boudreau, J. (1994). <u>Human Resource Management</u>. 7th Edition. Australia: Richard D. Irvin, Inc.

Ortigoza, Gabriel (2010). <u>Leadership Styles of Department Heads and Performance of Faculty Members at the Philippine Military Academy</u>. Printed in the USA.

Pigor, Paul & Charles Mayers (1973). <u>Personnel Administration: A Point of View and a Method</u>. 7th edition. McGraw-Hill, Kogakusha, Ltd., Japan.

Pope, John A. Jr. (1995). <u>Legal Problem Solver. A Quick-and-Easy Action Guide to the Law</u>. The Reader's Digest Association, Inc. Pleasantville, NY, U.S.A.

Pratt, K.J. & S.G. Bennett (1989). <u>Elements of Personnel Management</u>. Revised Second Edition. Van Nostrand Reinhold (International) Co., Ltd., London.

Reynes, Sara L. (1986). <u>Current Issues in Human Resource Management</u>. Business Publications Incorporated. Plano, Texas, USA.

Robbins, Stephen P. (1988). <u>Management</u>. 2nd Edition. Englewood Cliffs, New Jersey 07632. Prentice-Hall.

Schuller, Randal S. (1981) <u>Personnel and Human Resources Management</u>. West Publishing Company. St. Paul, Minnesota, USA.

Sison, Perfecto S. (1991). <u>Personnel and Human Resources Management</u>. 6th Edition. Rex Bookstore, Manila, Philippines.

Stahl, Oscar Glenn (1983). <u>Public Personnel Administration</u>. 8th Edition. New York: Harper & Row, Publishers, Inc.

Stoner, Jones A. F., and Freeman, R. Edward (1989). <u>Management</u>. 4th Edition. Englewood Cliffs. New Jersey: Prentice-Hall, Inc.

Terry, George R. (1977). <u>Principle of Management</u>. 7th Edition. Richard P. Erwin, Inc. USA.

Tomas, Andres (1991). <u>Human Resource Management - The Philippine Setting</u>. Philippines: New Day Publishers.

Manuals

AGREEMENT between Kaiser Permanente, Kaiser Foundation Hospitals, and The Permanente Medical Group, Inc. and California Nurses Association. CNA Headquarters, Oakland, California. 2018.

AFPM 10-1.

AFP Code of Ethics. 1991.

AFPM 10-2. <u>Armed Forces Training Management</u>. GHQ, AFP. 1974.

AFPM 12-2. <u>Armed Forces of the Philippines Manual</u>. The Adjutant General's Service. GHQ, AFP, 1993.

A Manual for Courts-Martial. Armed Forces of the Philippines. 1987.

Circular Number 22. <u>Officers Evaluations Rating</u>. GHQ, AFP, dated 14 October 1987.

Circular Number 16. <u>Enlisted Personnel Evaluation Marks</u>. Department of National Defense, General Headquarters. 13 September 1993.

Executive Order 237, series of 1957. <u>Prescribing Rules and Regulations Governing the Seniority, Appointment, Promotion, Elimination, and Utilization in Time of Emergency, of Officers of the Corps of Professors, Philippine Military Academy</u>. Presidential Museum and Library. Manila, Philippines. 13 February 1957.

Executive Order 284, Series of 1987. <u>Authorizing the Holding of other Government Offices or Positions by the Members of the Cabinet, Undersecretaries, Assistant Secretaries, and other Appointive Officials of the Executive Department Under Certain Conditions</u>. Presidential Management Staff. Manila, Philippines. 25 July 1987.

GO FORM 67-m Incl D to Circular Nr 22 dated 14 Oct 1987

<u>In Defense of the Philippines</u>. Defense Policy Paper. DND. Quezon City, 1998

<u>Military Professionalism in the Armed Forces of the Philippines</u>. MGEN Melchor P. Rosales, AFP.

<u>Omnibus Rules Implementing Book V of Executive Order no. 292</u>. Civil Service Laws. 1995.

Primer on the GSIS Act of 1997 (R.A. 8291).

Republic Act 291 – <u>An Act to Provide for the Procurement, Promotion, and Elimination of Regular Officers of the Armed Forces of the Philippines, and for other purposes.</u> Armed Forces Officer Personnel Act of 1948.

Internet

Chand, Smriti (2020). *Human Resources Management Operative Functions*. Retrieve from http://yourarticlelibrary.com/human-resources-management-operative-functions

Cursa (2018, November 12). *HR Basics: Human Resources Management in Organization*. Retrieved from http://www.cursa.app

HR Research – Research Topic in Human Resource Management. Retrieved from http://www.whatishumanresource.com/hrresearch-researchtopicinhumanresourcemanagement

Santana, M. *Coverage of HR Research*. Retrieve from http://businessmanagementideas.com/coverageofhrresearcharea

Rekha R (2020). Navigation: Industrial Relations. Retrieved form
http://www.economicsdiscussion.net/industrialrelations

Index

A

Abandonment · 96
absenteeism · 62, 69, 72, 90
accounting · 87, 88
Act · 17, 51, 56, 57, 58, 59, 76, 82, 83, 101
Adaptability · 29
Adequate · 56
admonished · 92
Advanced · 28, 31, 33
Advertising · 9, 10
AFP · 27, 28, 30, 32, 33, 34, 35, 38, 39, 40, 42, 43, 53, 67, 72, 76, 77, 78, 95, 100, 101
Allotment · 96, 97
analyzed · 4
Applicants · 9
appraisal · 12, 37, 38, 61, 62, 88, 90
Apprenticeship · 25
Armed Forces · 17, 21, 27, 28, 29, 67, 76, 100, 101
Armed Forces of the Philippines · 17, 21, 27, 76, 100, 101
Assessment centers · 48
Attrition · 11, 61
Audits · 88
Availability of Funds · 10
AWOL · 72, 95

B

Balanced · 56
Basic · 3, 30, 31, 33, 35, 108

C

Career · 19, 28, 33
Casual employee · 13
certificates · 87
challenge of management · vi
CIRCULAR · 43
Citizen · 21
Civil Rights Act · 51, 57, 82
Coaching · 26
combat operations · 31, 32
Combined training · 31
Commanding Officer · 44, 95
Commanding Officers · 67
commission · 28, 95, 108
Communication · 34, 35, 36
company level · 3
Comparative Approach · 90
compensation · 1, 5, 10, 48, 55, 56, 57, 58, 59, 71, 90
Compensation · 55, 56, 57, 58, 59

Complainant · 92, 93, 96
complaint · 92, 93, 95, 96, 97
Compliance Approach · 90
concepts of training · 30
Consistent · 62, 63
Contractual employee · 13
Corporate Level · 4
corporations · 4, 88
Correspondence · 24
Cost Effective · 56
counseling · 36, 40, 64, 69, 90
Counseling · 64
Courts-Martial · 67

D

Decree · 76
Decruitment · 11
defense · 21, 22, 27
Defense Department · 27
demotion · 50, 64, 68, 69
Demotion · 64, 68, 69
Dependents · 59
development · 1, 3, 4, 19, 20, 21, 22, 24, 25, 26, 27, 28, 29, 30, 31, 32, 37, 48, 52, 60, 68, 69, 70, 90
Development · 19, 21, 22, 23, 28, 33, 35, 60, 61, 62, 108
discharge · 53, 63, 64, 65, 72, 78
Discharge · 65, 77
Disciplinary action · 40
Discipline · 60, 65, 66, 67
Discrimination · 51, 57, 58, 82
Dismissal · 72
Dissatisfaction · 70
Domestic and foreign schooling · 27
Downward communication · 36

E

Early Retirement · 61, 71
Economic Liberalization · 82
Education and training · 27
Educational Institutions · 9
Employee benefits · 56
Employees · 4, 12, 13, 37, 48, 50, 52, 53, 59, 62, 63, 75, 98
Employer's Families · 9
Employment without a definite period · 13
Encouragement · 52
Enforce Rules · 63
enhancement · 21
Enlisted Personnel · 43, 100
Equitable · 56
Esprit de Corps · 29

About the Author

Gabriel C. Ortigoza was born on September 15, 1970, at the Philippine Military Academy Station Hospital in Baguio City. He is the youngest son of Marcelo Cruz Ortigoza, Sr., a retired Korean Veteran, and Daisy Celestial-Ortigoza, a retired teacher. He has a brother Marcelo, Jr. and a sister Sadie. Gabriel is married to Gemma Tankiamco and the couple has two sons whose biblical names are Gamiel and Gamaliel.

Gabriel finished his formal education in the Philippines: Elementary and High School at Southern Baptist College, Bachelor of Science in Nursing at Central Philippine University, Master in Management major in Public Management at University of the Philippines, Master of Public Administration at Baguio Central University, and Doctor of Philosophy in Management at the University of the Cordilleras.

On 16 March 1993, Gabriel was Called to Active Duty in the Regular Force of the Armed Forces of the Philippines with a military-grade of second lieutenant. His first assignment was at Southern Command in Zamboanga City. On 01 March 1995, two years later, Gabriel was reassigned to the Philippine Military Academy (PMA) in Baguio City.

In November of 1995, 2lt Gabriel C. Ortigoza O-11369 underwent and successfully finished one of the toughest military training in his life which is the Basic Airborne Course (BAC 72-95) at Special Forces School (Airborne) in Fort Magsaysay, Nueva Ecija.

On November 23, 2000, Captain Ortigoza joined the prestigious PMA Corps of Professors with a military-grade of captain and academic rank of assistant professor. Having conferred a master's degree before his appointment in the Corps, he should have been appointed with a military-grade of Major and academic rank of an associate professor based on Executive Order Nr 237 however PMA leadership believed he was too young, at age 30, to be appointed to such grade and rank.

Captain Ortigoza taught courses under the Department of Management and Department of Social Sciences such as principles of management, human resources management, public policy, constitution, economics, development management, and international relations. While at PMA, Captain Ortigoza was appointed to several positions such as Assistant Head of Department of Languages, Assistant Head of Department of Social Sciences, Officer-in-Charge of Department of Languages, Administrative Officer of PMA Research and Development Center, Protocol Officer, and Officer-in-Charge of PMA Disaster and Response Task Group.

In 2001, Captain Ortigoza was also appointed as Officer-in-Charge of the special PMA Entrance Examination (PMAEE) that was conducted in the cities of Davao, Cotabato, General Santos, and Koronadal. He brought PMAEE for the first time to his beloved town of Mlang in Cotabato Province.

On 18 September 2003, Captain Gabriel Ortigoza resigned his regular commission in the Corps of Professors to join his family in Sacramento, California.

Presently, Gabriel works as a registered nurse at Kaiser Permanente in Sacramento and serves as a clinical educator at the University of California Davis School of Nursing and California State University Sacramento School of Nursing.

www.ingramcontent.com/pod-product-compliance
Lightning Source LLC
Chambersburg PA
CBHW071530150726
48000CB00002B/749